A FATHER'S SECRET TREASURE BOX
REVEALS AN UNEXPECTED MAN

UNBOXING RAYMOND

A MEMOIR BY
LEN BOSWELL

Black Rose Writing | Texas

©2022 by Len Boswell
All rights reserved. No part of this book may be reproduced,
stored in a retrieval system or transmitted in any form or by
any means without the prior written permission of the
publishers, except by a reviewer who may quote brief
passages in a review to be printed in a newspaper,
magazine or journal.

The author grants the final approval for this literary
material.

First printing

This is a work of fiction. Names, characters, businesses,
places, events, and incidents are either the products of the
author's imagination or used in a fictitious manner. Any
resemblance to actual persons, living or dead, or actual
events is purely coincidental.

ISBN: 978-1-68433-948-8
PUBLISHED BY BLACK ROSE WRITING
www.blackrosewriting.com

Printed in the United States of America
Suggested Retail Price (SRP) $18.95

Unboxing Raymond is printed in Sabon

*As a planet-friendly publisher, Black Rose Writing does its best to
eliminate unnecessary waste to reduce paper usage and energy
costs, while never compromising the reading experience. As a result,
the final word count vs. page count may not meet common
expectations.

Parts of the present work appeared in slightly different versions in
Santa Takes a Tumble, copyright 2017 by Len Boswell.

To all I love without condition
To all I love without omission

Never doubt

And especially to Raymond, Dorothy, Kenny, and Nancy

"No memory is ever alone; it's at the end of a trail of memories, a dozen trails that each have their own associations."
–Louis L'Amour

"We do not know the true value of our moments until they have undergone the test of memory."
–Georges Duhamel

"Forgiving does not erase the bitter past. A healed memory is not a deleted memory. Instead, forgiving what we cannot forget creates a new way to remember. We change the memory of our past into a hope for our future."
–Lewis B. Smedes

"What was silent in the father speaks in the son, and often I found in the son the unveiled secret of the father."
–Friedrich Nietzsche

"I wouldn't describe myself as lacking in confidence, but I would just say that-the ghosts you chase you never catch."
–John Malkovich

PREFACE

Sometimes we put people in boxes. They hurt us in some way, and into a box they go, sometimes forever. Such was the case with my father. I put him in the Emotional Abuser Box and kept him there, hating him every day, even beyond his death. And I was certain he hated me.

Or so I thought.

But then a mysterious wooden box arrived in the mail from my late sister's estate, a box wrapped in a bright blue ribbon with a tag that read, "Ray Boswell's Treasure Box." And that changed *everything*.

The contents of the box brought back a flood of memories, some painful and some poignant, but most joyful. So this book is not a blow-by-blow, woe-is-me account of emotional abuse. It is, rather, a rediscovery of my father, one treasure at a time, to form a redemptive portrait of the man in full. I hope to show you the often funny, sometimes poignant, sometimes horrific life of a self-employed upholsterer, pigeon fancier, and believer in ghosts and angels, as well as give you a glimpse of times long gone, when horses and streetcars ruled Washington, D.C., and Raymond ran barefoot through its streets.

Along the way there will be shocks and surprises, for you and for me, but the memories will be more fond than fraught. And there will be more laughter than tears. As you will see from the chapter titles, I take after my mother, using humor to fight pain. Our unstated family motto was *you've got to laugh, or you'd cry*.

But back to the box.

The box reflects the man. Stout, sturdy, and simple of purpose and design, it is both elegant in its simplicity and boastful of all the complexities that made it so. Each corner has been rounded and dovetailed by a craftsman who knew his way around wood. Delicate brass hinges, darkened with age, adorn the lid, which is held fast by an ornate brass clasp, suggesting the box's intended use was to hold a woman's everyday jewelry.

But perhaps not. Our craftsman has added a brass carry handle, suggesting the box may have been the home to a precious if arcane tool of some sort, now long gone. Even so, at no more than two hands long by one hand wide and no deeper than a maiden's pinky, the walnut-stained box seems inadequate to hold the treasures and memories of a man who lived to be eighty-three. And yet the treasures inside reveal a wider, much larger world, filled with memories and events too long compressed in space and time.

Some say that life is like a finely woven tapestry that depicts scenes from our life and times. I think that's fine if you know everything about a life. But I don't know everything about Raymond. No, I am more of the school that suggests life is like a jigsaw puzzle. It's complex and filled with strangely shaped pieces, all of which only fit together in one way. And often, we don't have all the pieces. My hope is to assemble enough of those pieces I do have to give readers a glimpse of my father—and to know him better myself.

Let's begin the puzzle and our treasure hunt. Forgive me, father, but it is now time for you to be unboxed.

UNBOXING
RAYMOND

1
THINGS, WONDERFUL THINGS!

The blue ribbon slides off the box easily. It had been placed there by my dear sister, who was known and celebrated for her ribbons and glitter and stickers and balloons. She had kept our father's treasures safe through the years, and now with her passing, that job has turned to me.

I lift the lid and offer an unexpected gasp as memory-wrapped treasures leap out at me, each seemingly shouting, "Me first!" Coins, jewelry, and true mysteries lie in a jumble in four boxed-off sections. The first section, which is narrow and runs the length of the box, seems well suited for necklaces or perhaps long tools of unknown purpose. Behind it are three more rectangular sections, each of unique dimensions, though one is more than twice the size of the other two and occupies the center of the box. The smaller compartments to either side are clearly intended for smaller items, perhaps earrings or rings, or even nails or screws.

Whatever the original purpose of the box was, it is clear from the markings on the inside lid that it was once used to sell small items. I recognize my father's hand, so it doesn't take me long to parse out what he has written in chalk: "80—25¢" and "144—10¢." It appears that the original price for one item was originally "146—10¢," but my father had apparently changed his mind, thinking the pricing too generous.

I take a deep breath. I thought that I would immediately dive into the contents of the box, but the chalk message has catapulted me back in time. My father, a self-employed upholsterer, is hunched over a sofa he has just brought into the shop, a building without right angles he has built in our backyard from scrap lumber, and seemingly held up by nothing more than air quotes.

He is forty-four, and still a fine figure of a man, though his belly is showing signs of rebellion. His once black hair is showing signs of gray at the temple, but his eyes, pale as a winter sky, still hold their hypnotic power. My mother always said it was his eyes that captured her, and he likes to think they could still capture any woman.

As always on these hot summer days, he is dressed in gray cotton slacks and a white, sweat-stained tee-shirt. He's already stripped the original fabric from the sofa, and is now draping new fabric over it. He tilts his head this way and that, trying to decide where to make the cuts in the fabric necessary to make the sofa a sofa again.

There seems to be more art than science to the way he strikes the fabric with his chalk, each mark denoting where to cut to get the best fit. A mark here for an arm, a mark there for a curve in the back. Mark, mark, mark— done. He grabs the fabric and moves to his cutting table, which is really nothing more than a piece of plywood resting on overly tall sawhorses.

He suddenly stops and looks at me. "Is that what I think it is?" he says, pointing at the floor.

I look down, and there in all its splendor is a silver dollar. I don't need to be asked what to do next. I am on it in a flash, visions of candy and milkshakes in my head, and maybe a trip to the Coral Hills Theater, where for twenty-five cents I could see a new episode of Flash Gordon and a war movie starring Audie Murphy.

But I can't pick it up. It's a practical joke, a fake coin that you nail to the floor to frustrate anyone who happens upon it. And, of course, my father is laughing at me now, so there's nothing I can do but join in.

I shake off the memory. Let's get back to the box, and the *real* treasures.

2
LOOK AT IT THIS WAY

I open the box again and take out the largest item—a pair of rimless glasses added to the box after his death—and I hear the argument all over again. We have fast-forwarded to the 1980s. Raymond is now well into his seventies. His hair is thin and gray, and the athletic body that once excited young women is now hunched and thick. His legs, which once earned him wins in neighborhood swimming contests, are now thin as twigs. The immediate impression you get of the man is that he looks like a potato supported by toothpicks. Of course, this is not the man he sees in the mirror. He still thinks he's a vibrant young man and is having a terrible time coming to grips with aging, particularly his failing eyesight. My mother, Dorothy, a graying woman barely over five feet tall, is looking up at him, trying to explain why a customer is so upset with the work he has done reupholstering her chair.

Dorothy, the love of his life, is his counselor and guide. When it comes to things small and large, she is the only one who can get his ear or get him to do the right thing. At times, I thought of her as the lion tamer in our household, the only person who could control the lion and his growl.

He can't understand what she is trying to tell him, because his whole work life has been devoted to perfection. He is not just a self-employed upholsterer; he is an upholsterer who doesn't advertise, a man whose business is based on word-of-mouth praise for his work. In his best years, no pattern could defeat him. Stripes, chevrons, and ornate brocades were his bread and butter, the work so seamless the patterns seemed to be painted on the chair or sofa. But now, when not even a squint could keep patterns straight, the words are less kind, and business is shrinking.

My mother stamps her foot and leans toward him, hands on hips. "I *told* you it was wrong. The pattern was all skee-jawed. But no, you wouldn't listen to *me*."

My father is livid. "There is nothing *wrong* with the job. It's *perfect*."

The argument continues, exclamation marks flying around the room. He will call her "Nuisance" now, the pet name he used whenever he was upset with her. But she will stand her ground, because she is right, and as was the case with most arguments, she will win.

The glasses, the first he has ever worn, prove her case. As soon as he puts them on, a whole new world—*a new whole world*—comes into view. His mouth is open as he turns in a circle, trying to take everything in.

Finally, he stops and looks at my mother. "Damn, you're getting old."

The punch to his arm comes before her smile.

3
YOU KNOW WHAT I MEAN?

It is just another day for the wider world. Lucille Ball, one of seven Goldwyn Girls, is on the road promoting Eddie Cantor's new film, *Roman Scandals*, one of her earliest film appearances. Joan Baez and Bart Starr are sliding down the chute to their first day on the planet. The American flag has forty-eight stars. President Roosevelt is in the White House, celebrating the turning point in the Great Depression, thrilled that unemployment has dropped to 22 percent. The U.S. population has grown to 126 million, about 200 million less than today's population. At the local markets, hand-plucked, freshly butchered spring chickens are selling for twenty cents a pound. J. Edgar Hoover and the FBI are about to end the careers of celebrity criminals John Dillinger, Bonnie and Clyde, Pretty Boy Floyd, and Baby Face Nelson. Meanwhile, Adolph Hitler is consolidating power and is about to declare himself Führer.

But as the yellowed piece of paper I've pulled from the box suggests, it is anything but just another day for Raymond. For starters, it's his twenty-fifth birthday, which should be reason enough to set the date apart from others. But wait, there's more. The old marriage license reveals that he and my mother have chosen this day to take the vows that no man or woman would put asunder during their fifty-eight years of marriage.

My mother taps me on the shoulder from the beyond. "Don't forget to tell them it was snowing to beat the band."

Well, nothing to be overly alarmed about. By the time the brief ceremony was over, the cars parked along the street—mostly old Fords and Chevys, with the odd Durant, Sheridan, and Hudson Super-Six thrown in—are covered in a light blanket of snow.

My mother taps harder. "Don't forget the Duessy!"

It was her dream car. In fact, everyone's dream car back then. Sleek as an arrow, a mansion on wheels, the brand new 1934 Duesenberg Model J was part carriage, part locomotive, and part vector to the future. But today it is speeding past them, its straight-eight engine growling, and they both wonder on this day for dreaming whether it is a harbinger of better things to come, or just another tease.

I shake off the memory.

Something about the date gives me pause enough to double-check my mother's date of birth, and then there she is again, standing in the kitchen doorway, reflecting on her marriage day.

"Your father was a cradle robber, for sure," she says with an impish double pump of her eyebrows.

At the time, I thought nothing of it. But now I'm faced with the fact that she was just three months over seventeen when she got married. Or as the Beatles would sing, "She was just seventeen." That means my 24-year-old father must certainly have been dating a 16-year-old girl, a fact that might elicit more than a few "ewwws" from people today.

Or even back then. I checked the statistics, and back then, in 1934, marrying so young was definitely not the norm. The median age at marriage was 24.3 for men and 21.3 for women. But clearly, a man on one side of the curve was dating a girl on the other side.

Still, the heart wants what the heart wants, right? And remember, "The way she looked was way beyond compare," so who can fault him? As a product of that union, certainly not me. What I'm left with, though, is the realization that I know very little about either of them pre-me. That's a void of thirty-three years of my father's life and twenty-six of my mother's.

What I do remember, though, comes at me full throttle, encouraging me to set the box aside for a time and tell you what I do know about their early years, the things they told me over and over again, so I'd remember.

Ah, let's start with the crystal clear Potomac River. It's 1915 and my father, age 6, is about to take his early morning swim. All he has to do is tiptoe from the room he shares with his still-sleeping brothers Stanley, George, and Fred, fumble for the fishing rod in the downstairs closet, and ease the front door open without waking the rest of the household, including his mother, father, and eight sisters.

Once outside, he begins to run, picking up speed with every barefoot step.

4
SEEING BOTTOM

I was fifteen when my father, Raymond, decided he much preferred the idea of free labor to another less attractive idea, namely paying the guy across the street, Eddie Kite, to help him deliver furniture. More often than not, our route would take us down Pennsylvania Avenue, through the Anacostia area of Washington, D.C., and across the Sousa Bridge, which spanned the muddy Anacostia River.

Every time we crossed, whether coming or going, my father would mention the deleterious effect of time on the river.

"I used to swim here from the time I was six. The water was clear as tap water. You could see the fish, you could see the bottom."

Yes, it was a different time, and a different place. Little of Raymond's childhood world in Southwest Washington remains. Most of it, including his boyhood home, was bulldozed over in the 1950s as part of a government reclamation project, an attempt to revitalize the area at the expense of the poor people who lived there. Eminent domain ruled the day and scattered the residents.

Back then, pre-bulldozers, Southwest Washington was the poorest section of the city, with dilapidated row houses and single-family homes, most with outhouses of questionable construction and utility. The westernmost section along the river was the home to white immigrants, mostly from Britain and Germany. To the east, just beyond 4th Street (which was actually 4½ Street at that time) were the homes of poor blacks. Each area could lay claim to a famous singer: Al Jolson to the west, Marvin Gaye to the east.

Raymond's house, a large two-story home near the intersection of 6th Street and Maine Avenue, had four bedrooms, three of which would have been shared with his eight sisters and three brothers. I visited the house on moving day, just hours before it would be bulldozed into oblivion. At the time, only Grandma Daisey and my Aunt Ruth, her constant companion, lived there. My lasting memories of the place are the heavy curtains that hung from every window, furniture festooned with antimacassars, their nameless, round-as-a-ball cat, the incredible heat blasting from their coal furnace, and the multi-paned French doors that led from the dining room out to Daisey's garden and the outhouse.

But let's go further back in time.

On any summer morning in 1915, when Raymond was six, you would find him racing barefoot out the front door, fishing pole in hand, and heading in one of two directions: west toward The Wharf and the waters of the Washington Channel of the Potomac River or south toward the Anacostia River. He could have split the difference and headed southwest, but that would have meant fishing and swimming in the confluence of the

Potomac and the Anacostia, and that was tricky, and dangerous.

On most days, he chose the area near The Wharf, where if his fishing luck was good, he could sell part of his haul at the Maine Street Fish Market, enough perhaps for a streetcar ride to the many attractions of downtown Washington.

Fishing was what he did second, though. The first order of business was a swim in the river. He didn't have a bathing suit, of course, but he was already shoeless and his mode of dress—shorts and an undershirt—served him well.

Raymond always claimed he could have been an Olympic swimmer, because he "swam better than most fish." We'll have to take his word on that, because he was never a competitive swimmer, except for friend-against-friend dares. But at six years old, you'd have to be pretty good to deal with the Potomac and its currents.

"Partly, it was fun," he told me. "But partly it was to spy on the fish. When I came out, I knew exactly where to drop my line."

And sometimes, like this particular ride across the bridge, he would admit that he wasn't there just for the fishing and the swimming. He was there to meet his childhood friend Darla, who lived even closer to The Wharf and could "swim to beat the band."

He'd tear up every time he mentioned her, because three years later, in the autumn of 1918, he would lose her to the Spanish Flu, along with his sweet older sister Violet, who was known forever after as Baby Violet.

Between October 1, 1918 and February 1, 1919, some 33,719 Washington residents fell ill with influenza, with

2,895 of them succumbing to the disease, Darla and Violet among them. It was a particularly bad strain of flu. There were the normal flu symptoms of fever, nausea, aches and diarrhea, and many developed severe pneumonia attacks. For those that wouldn't make it, dark spots would appear on the cheeks and then they'd turn blue, suffocating from a lack of oxygen as their lungs filled with a frothy, bloody substance.

At this point, Raymond would wipe away his tears, accelerate over the bridge, make his way around the streetcar terminal, and head for downtown.

"Here we go," he said, fumbling in his pocket for the scrap of paper that identified our destination. "Seventeenth and Columbia Road."

It didn't take me long to figure out what story would come next. We were headed to an apartment building just a block away from one of the worst disasters in Washington history: the collapse of the Knickerbocker Theater during the blizzard of 1922. My father's next words did not surprise me.

"It was horrific."

5
THE KNICKERBOCKER

From the outside, the Knickerbocker Theater, a three-story, brick structure that curved gracefully around the corner of 18th and Columbia Road, looked fine.

"It looked like a tall slice of pie," said Raymond. "You'll see. It's called the Ambassador Theater now."

I start to tell him *I know, you've told this story before,* but he's already moving deeper into the story. When he arrived on the scene, his first thought was that his brother George had played a dirty trick on him, sending him off on a miles-long trek through the deep snow for nothing. But he could tell from the number of people surrounding the theater, particularly the policemen, firemen, and army troops, that something terrible had indeed happened.

"And the screams. God, the screams. Not just from the rescue workers, but from people still trapped under the debris."

The heavy wet snow had started to fall on the evening of January 27, 1922, and would continue to fall through January 29, accumulating an estimated 28 inches of snow, the largest snowfall in Washington history. Raymond had spent all of January 28 building snowmen and snow forts and participating in running snowball fights with his brothers throughout his neighborhood.

"We didn't have boots, of course," he said, "so we had to go back inside every hour or so to dry our shoes and socks on the radiator."

"Yes, the mismatched socks," I say, and he gives me a scolding look, unhappy that I have interrupted.

"Anyway," he says, "it was eerie. The building looked fine, but the roof had collapsed."

He never told me why it collapsed, or who was to blame. It's easy to say that the weight of the snow was the culprit. Washington had never seen such a snow, and it was a wet, heavy snow. But there was more to it than that. While the building was being constructed, the builder asked the architect to make a change in the structural steel he had selected to bear the weight of the reinforced concrete slabs that would hover over those 1700 theater seats. Steel was scarce, and expensive, following the War to End All Wars, so it was not an unreasonable request. By using lighter, less robust steel girders, they could save time and expense. The architect relented, on the understanding that the change would have to be approved by building inspectors.

What the architect failed to do, however, was to recalculate the load-bearing strength of the new steel. If he had, the tragedy could have been prevented, a fact that gnawed at the architect and led to his ultimate suicide.

But there was still more to it than the wrong steel. One of the quirky characteristics of the clay blocks used in the construction of the supporting walls was that they tended to expand and contract dramatically with changes in temperature. When the blocks expanded, the girders *resting* on them—that's right, they weren't attached in any way—would inch toward the inside of the building, and when they contracted, the girders would inch back—but not all the way back. In the five years since the building had been constructed, the girders had worked themselves closer and closer to the inside edge. A little weight was all that was needed to make one of the corner girders fall, which took down all the others in rapid succession, the roof collapsing first on the balcony, and then to the ground floor.

Estimates of the number of people who had come in from the storm to see the comedy "Get-Rich-Quick Wallingford" ranged from 300 to 1700 to standing room only. And to those numbers, you'd have to add in the full orchestra accompanying the silent film.

My father has now reached his favorite part of the story. "The first person to realize something bad was about to happen was a coal miner, can you believe it? He said there was a cracking sound, a sound that reminded him of the same sound a mine tunnel makes just before it collapses."

The man had leaped up, made his way to the aisle, and raced for the lobby, reaching it just as the balcony collapsed behind him. In the end, 98 people were killed and 133 injured. Most of the people who survived had been sitting under the balcony. Alerted by the sound of the initial collapse, many had been able to race to the safety of the lobby before the balcony itself collapsed. But not all.

"Bodies were lined up on the ground, covered with army blankets." He shivered. "I saw a policeman carrying a single leg."

He had reached the end of the story, or at least all that he ever shared with me, so I dutifully provided the final word: "Wow."

We drive on in silence until blocks and blocks later Raymond sticks his arm out the car window and points at a building.

"There it is, the Ambassador. Outside looks almost the same."

At this point, I am obliged to give the storyteller another "wow," so I do.

A decade later, unable to compete with the inroads made by television and the big studio theaters, the Ambassador is torn down to make way for a bank.

But my father is not thinking about that right now. He has caught sight of our destination, and we both have the same reaction. "Oh, shit."

The apartment building looms before us. My father checks his little scrap of paper. "Damn, Nuisance has done it again. It's on the eighth floor!"

I roll my eyes, thinking of what lies ahead. My father will not use elevators, but that's another story.

6
THE ELEVATOR

He has no name. He could be a John or a Lester or a Bill. He has no age. He could be young or middle-aged or ready for retirement. He has no physical description. He could be tall or short, fat or thin. He could have black hair or ginger.

Whoever he was, his death in 1934 changed my father's life forever, and even before we were born, affected the lives of me, my older sister, my younger brother, and my mother.

But I get ahead of myself.

When Raymond married Dorothy, he was working as a staff upholsterer at Hotel Washington, a posh hotel in downtown Washington (now a W Hotel). Jobs were scarce during the Depression, so if you had one, you did everything you could to hold onto it. For Raymond and his fellow upholsterer—let's call him Al—that meant "making work." They would use their pass keys to enter empty hotel rooms, where they would damage furniture with lit cigarettes, tear loose seams and fringe, and otherwise make repair a good idea. The cleaning staff would find the damage, blame it on the last occupant, and notify the manager, who would then send for Raymond and Al. It may not have been ethical, but it was a scheme that kept food on the table during trying times.

Until.

There is always an *until*, that moment when things change, for good or ill, and life tumbles in an unexpected direction. For Raymond, it was a call from the manager. There was a damaged sofa in Room 1011, and it needed fixing. The previous guest had apparently burned a whole in it and had left without reporting the problem.

After a brief back-and-forth about the evil that guests do, Raymond hung up the phone and gave Al a sly smile. "Seems we have a damaged sofa in 1011."

Al returned the smile, tamped out his cigarette on the bottom of his shoe, and followed Raymond down the hall to the freight elevator, which was used by all the craftsmen and the cleaning staff.

After propping open the door to 1011, Raymond and Al picked up the sofa and carted it out into the hallway, setting it down briefly to close and lock the door to the room. Then they proceeded down the hall to the elevator, Al in the lead, walking backwards, with my father at the other end, giving instructions.

"Here we are," said my father.

"Right," said Al, resting the edge of the sofa briefly on one hip in order to turn and open the manual elevator door.

That's when *The Until* arrived with lasting horror. Al lifted the sofa off his hip and began backing into the elevator. The problem was the elevator was on the basement level, in use by the cleaning staff. Al stepped backwards and fell ten stories to his death, the sofa following, Raymond looking on in horror.

My mother always referred to this incident as "the breakdown," for surely it was that. My father was broken, a nervous wreck for years afterward. *The Until* was merciless. The once easygoing and affable young Raymond was now moody, depressed, and withdrawn, and given to violent outbursts, outbursts that would eventually be directed at me and my brother, Kenny. Raymond never held a job again, living the rest of his life as a self-employed upholsterer. They didn't have a fancy name for it back then, but it's clear as I think of it now that my father was suffering from posttraumatic stress disorder (PTSD), which would go untreated for the rest of his life. That fact gives me pause now, chastens me for my hatred of him growing up. He just couldn't help himself or control himself.

Raymond never referred to *The Until*. The most that he would ever offer was that he was claustrophobic and therefore couldn't ride in elevators, including this one, years later, at the apartment building on Columbia Road.

I knew by then that it was pointless to ask if I could ride the elevator up to the customer's apartment. That was forbidden, so I joined him on the eight-story climb up the switchback concrete stairs. The number of steps between floors always varied. Sometimes it was forty, sometimes it was fifty, and sometimes it was an odd number like thirty-seven. At any rate, counting helped distract me from the pain in my thighs and the sound of my father's labored breathing as we climbed on and on.

This could take a while, so let's get back to the box and see what new treasure we can find.

7
BUCKLE UP!

The next treasure I pull from Raymond's box is all too familiar. It's a square, somewhat tarnished silver belt buckle, monogrammed with the letter "R" and filigreed with ornate branches and flowers around its square surface. It's a small buckle as buckles go, but it is just right for the slim leather belts men wore in the 1950s.

I flip the buckle over, and find that it was manufactured by a company called Giant Grip. The company seems unusually ethical. They have taken great care to let the buckle owner know that the little swivel gizmo that attaches the buckle to the belt is made of base metal, not silver.

The buckle, combined with a slim black leather belt of varying length, depending on Raymond's eating habits, is his go-to dress-up belt. He wears it every time he wears his suit, which is whenever he goes to meet with a new customer.

So as we trudge up the stairs to the eighth-floor apartment, each carrying ring-bound fabric samples weighing about thirty pounds, I need only look to my left to see my father in his "estimate suit." The suit is blue and as rumpled and stained as any suit could be that has never seen the inside of a dry cleaning establishment. On off days, it's part of the pile of clothes at the end of his and Dorothy's bed.

Occasionally, if there's time and my mother's in the mood, she will take a hot flatiron to it to smooth out the worst wrinkles. But Raymond is hesitant to let her do that. His previous suit, which was dark brown and made him look like a bear, ended its life in flames at the hand of my mother's flatiron.

An equally rumpled tie and a shirt of suspect whiteness completes his outfit, along with matching trousers held up by the silver-buckled belt.

I don't look much better. I am dressed in jeans and a tee-shirt I've worn for several days. Cleanliness and godliness were never too close together in our house. Not that we didn't want to be clean. It was just that the washing machine was always broken and the water pipes to the bathtub only supplied a trickle of water. Drawing a cold bath could be an all-day affair, so we usually made do with a quick scrub of our armpits with a wash rag.

So, imagine that you are a wealthy woman waiting for the arrival of the upholsterer, a man your best friend says does excellent work at bargain rates. Now imagine opening the door to see Raymond and me standing there in the hallway, sweating profusely from our climb.

Yes, you would take a step back and wonder whether to slam the door and run. They invariably did the first part, stepping back in alarm, a hand to their chest, mouth agape. But then they'd recover. The friend said bargain rates, so perhaps the risk would be worth it.

We step inside, and my father, who imagines himself a ladies' man, begins his flirtation, complimenting her and her apartment as he pulls out his yellow measuring tape and makes his way to the sofa she is pointing at, all with the outlandish flare of W. C. Fields.

"This one, is it?"

"Yes," she says, "I just hate the fabric, and we're going to repaint the apartment, so I thought maybe something in a rich burgundy, perhaps with gold threads throughout. Nothing too fancy, mind. Not flowers, certainly."

"No," says Raymond. "Not flowers."

He motions her to sit down on another sofa, and then turns to me. "Lenny, help her with the sample books while I do my measuring."

I nod, and lug the two sample books over to the woman and set them down on her coffee table.

"I think the bigger book there will have what you're looking for," says Raymond. "Have a look-see while I finish with my calculations."

A period of silence ensues. The woman flips through the samples, alternately nodding or shaking her head. My father does his dance around the sofa, arms outstretched with the tape to get its measure. Then he stops and suddenly turns back to the woman. "What color are you going to paint the walls?"

She brightens at the thought of discussing her color choice. "Oh, a wonderful yellowish beige."

Raymond looks at the walls, and grunts. "Yellow, huh?"

"Yellow*ish*," she says. "But more beige."

Raymond nods. "That should work well." He points at the sample book. "Take a look at the brocade about halfway through."

Through all this, I stand quietly away from the action, taking in the apartment, which is pin neat and at the edge of opulence, totally unlike our home, which given Raymond's inclinations, looks like a yard sale that has moved indoors.

"There," says Raymond, finally. "We'll need seven yards of material in the sofa's current configuration. But if you'd like me to tuft the back to give it a more elegant appearance, we'll need about three yards more, plus an allowance for tacks and buttons and sewing. And labor and delivery, of course."

He had her at *tufting*. "Ooh, tufting. That would be wonderful." She holds up a sample. "Would tufting work with this fabric?"

My father walks over to take a closer look. "Yes, that will work fine."

She gives him a mock cringe. "And how much will all this cost?"

"Hold on," says Raymond. He pulls out the same scrap of paper with the address, flips it over, and begins his "maths" with a snub of a pencil.

"Oh, I hope it's not too much. Fred set a limit for me."

Raymond is still calculating. "Uh-huh," he says absently.

"And if the price is right, perhaps I can get that hideous chair over there done as well."

My father takes a quick glance at the chair, then turns to the woman. "Okay, the sofa will be ninety bucks. And if you like, I can do the chair for another thirty."

I can tell by the woman's barely suppressed smile that she is over the moon with the price. In fact, I'm sure she'll be on the phone to her friend the moment we leave the apartment, promising to take her out for cocktails. An estimate from any other upholsterer in the area would have been almost twice as much.

"Both, please, both."

"Great," says Raymond. "Lenny and I will just take our sample books back to the van, and then we'll be back up for the sofa and chair."

"Wonderful," she says, standing to shake my father's hand. "I'll alert management so they can clear the elevator for you."

My father blanches. "Um, that won't be necessary. The surest way to damage a piece of furniture is to force it into an elevator. We'll take the stairs."

The woman is incredulous. "The stairs? But it must weigh a ton."

"No matter, ma'am. We're used to it. Right, Lenny?"

I can only nod.

8
SOFA ON THE STAIRS

My father was a magician of sorts when it came to spatial relationships. Length, width, and depth were his playthings. Although he was an advocate of the maxim *measure twice cut once*, the estimation dance he did with his tape measure was more for show; he wanted customers to think he was being precise in his measurements. And he was, even though he could look at a sofa or chair from across a room and pronounce, "Six yards for that one, and nine for that one." And he'd be right. Every time.

The same was true when it came to moving furniture through doorways. If you've ever tried to move a large sofa into or out of your home or apartment, you know that sometimes the solution can be a real head-scratcher. Not so for my father. Before we had even come into the woman's apartment, my father had assessed what needed to be done, and his first sight of the sofa had confirmed his calculations.

Which is why when we trudged back up the sixteen flights of stairs to the eighth floor, we brought along a drop cloth. We weren't so much worried about the fabric on the sofa—it was all going to be replaced—but we were worried about damaging the sofa's wooden legs.

Raymond knew how to fix scratches and scrapes in wood, but using the drop cloth would save him hours in the end.

"We'll need to turn the sofa on end and work the back through first, turning it slightly as we go. Then, once the top has cleared, we'll need to twist it round and tip it down a bit to slide the rest of the sofa out—but just. We can't come too far into the hallway or we'll get stuck making the turn. That hallway is tight, so follow my lead."

"Right," I say, not following a word of what he has just said.

I did not inherit his skill in spatial relationships, a fact my wife points out every time I attempt to put away the groceries. I guess there's something in my genetic makeup that makes me think an elephant can fit inside a thimble. It should be able to, right?

The plan works perfectly, although I can see the anger building in my father as I struggle to make sense of his instructions. I know that once we are out of earshot and moving down the stairs, I will be the recipient of a steady stream of obscenities, linked to words like *fool, idiot,* and—his favorite—*no-account bastard.*

Part of the stream of verbal abuse is prompted by my struggles with space, part by Raymond's problem with anger management, and part by the physical disparity between him and me. Raymond, now in his mid-forties, is barrel-chested and robust, while I am rail thin, like the kid in the old muscle-building ad who gets sand kicked in his face while a bathing beauty oohs and ahs at the muscular moron doing the kicking. In short, manhandling a sofa down sixteen flights of stairs is not an easy task for me. I turn this way, when I should turn that, again and again, each miscue prompting a new expletive from Raymond.

Fortunately, by the time we reach the fourth floor, we have settled into a rhythm Raymond deems acceptable. He is quiet now, and has moved on from his violent outbursts as if a switch has been thrown.

"Okay, we can do this," he says.

He has forgotten about his outburst, but each of his words has insinuated itself into my soul, making me ever meeker and ever quieter. There will be years ahead when I barely say more than a few words a day. But for all the negative effects of emotional abuse, I am stronger in at least one way: I am a survivor. Hit me with your best shot, and I'll just keep standing back up. Get in my face, and I'll just stare back at you, steel against steel. I've been attacked by a master, so you really don't stand a chance. If necessary, I will beat my face into your fists until you drop from exhaustion.

Raymond suddenly breaks his silence again. "We'll need to stop at Bedelle's to pick up the fabric, but then let's go to Stephanson's."

He is referring to Stephanson's Bakery, a landmark in Anacostia for years, now long gone. People would line up on Sundays to buy their still-warm coconut cream pies for Sunday dinner. And bags and bags of their famous tea cookies, which were so addictive that few people made it out of the bakery before breaking into the black-and-white checkerboard bag, which more than likely would be all that they'd have left when they arrived home.

The forty dollar deposit he received from the customer is already burning a hole in his pocket. Back then, we lived in alternating states of feast and famine, with an emphasis on famine. Whenever money came into the house, it went right back out, in gushes, household budget be damned.

But this was not just Raymond's problem. The whole family participated. When he mentioned the bakery, I immediately started dreaming of spending the rest of my Saturday at the movies. My brother, sister, and mother would have already anticipated his stop at the bakery, and would be lying in wait for him as soon as he walked through the door, each hoping for enough money to get or do some wonderful thing.

The stop at Bedelle's only took a few minutes. From there, we headed back down Pennsylvania Avenue, past the Capitol, across the Sousa Bridge, and into the parking lot of Stephanson's Bakery. The walls and floors inside the bakery were made of black and white ceramic subway tile. Once inside, you had the feeling that you were playing a three-dimensional game of checkers.

Raymond came out of the bakery carrying two boxes, one holding his favorite pie, Lemon Meringue, and the other holding my mother's favorite pie: mincemeat. They were both "cripple pies," pies with damaged crusts that the bakery sold at a discount. I managed to come out with a little bag of tea cookies and, more important, the change from the transaction, enough for a grand afternoon at the Coral Hills Theater.

I was already halfway through the bag of cookies when we made the left turn out of the parking lot and back onto Pennsylvania Avenue. Seconds later, we drove past The Highland Theater, which was showing a double feature of "The Tingler" and "Plan 9 from Outer Space," which only whet my appetite further for an afternoon at the movies. From there, we continued up Pennsylvania

Avenue, going up and down two large hills before the avenue crested at Dupont Village. Then it was down one final hill to a left turn onto Southern Avenue, which formed one of the boundaries between D.C. and Maryland. A mile later we made a right-hand turn onto R Street, taking us into Bradbury Heights, Maryland, where we lived. My mother, sister, and brother were sitting on the front stoop, waiting for us.

Before the car rolls to a stop and my family catches sight of the black-and-white pie boxes my father will hold up high, I thought I'd let you in on a couple of secrets, or at least what used to be secrets: the recipes for Stephanson's tea cookies and their coconut cream pie. Enjoy!

STEPHANSON'S BUTTER TEA COOKIES
1/4 pound best-quality butter
1 1/2 cups shortening with some animal fat (important)
1 cup very fine granulated sugar
2 eggs
Pinch of salt
Pinch of nutmeg
1 teaspoon vanilla
4 cups hard wheat flour

Beat butter, shortening, sugar and 1 cup of flour until nice and creamy. Add eggs, one at a time, beating well after each addition. Add salt, nutmeg and vanilla, and beat well. Add remaining 3 cups of flour by hand.

Place dough (or part of it, depending on size of pastry bag) into a pastry bag fitted with a No. 6-B tube. Lightly grease pan or use parchment paper. Press dough out for cookies about the size of a silver dollar. Bake in 325- to 350-degree oven for 7-8 minutes or until baked but not too brown.

STEPHANSON'S COCONUT CUSTARD PIE

There is some disagreement about which of the following recipes is the actual secret recipe. Try it both ways.

Recipe One

1 cup sugar
1/2 teaspoon salt
1 teaspoon cornstarch
4 eggs
3 cups milk
1 teaspoon vanilla
1 cup coconut
1 deep 9-inch or 10-inch pie crust, uncooked

Combine sugar, salt and cornstarch. Beat eggs and add to dry ingredients. Beat in milk and vanilla. Sprinkle coconut over bottom of pie crust, then pour in the egg mixture. Bake 1 hour at 400 degrees, or reduce oven to 350 degrees if top is browning before the bottom crust has cooked thoroughly.

Recipe Two

1 (9 inch) deep dish pie shell
1 cup coconut (toast ½ coconut, optional)

1 cup sugar

Dash salt

1 teaspoon cornstarch

4 eggs

3 cups half and half (may substitute one (12 oz.) can coconut milk plus ¾ cup (6 oz.) half and half)

Dash vanilla

1. Preheat oven to 350 degrees
2. If toasting coconut, spread on cookie sheet, bake 3-4 minutes. Watch closely; burns quickly. An amber color is desirable. Toasting ½ coconut and leaving ½ fresh is nice. If coconut is hard/stale, first soak in warm milk until rehydrated. Drain well. If toasting, cool. Spread in bottom of pie crust.
3. Combine sugar, salt and cornstarch
4. Whisk or beat eggs. Combine half and half (or coconut milk/half and half) with eggs.
5. Add vanilla and sugar mixture.
6. Pour egg mix over coconut in crust. Place pie on rimmed baking sheet.
7. Bake in middle or lower half oven about 1 hour. Reduce oven to 325 degrees if top is browning too quickly. Pie is done when the middle "soufflés" above the edges.
7. That's it! Can you believe how easy that is? Never tell.
8. Serve with warm commercial hot fudge sauce (Optional: add dash of rum or brandy and/or sprinkle of cayenne pepper to fudge sauce when warm)

9
THE HOUSE THAT RAYMOND BUILT

The pin-on button is so big, I can't believe it has taken me this long to pull it out of the box. It's a simple, but large, button that proudly proclaims the name of our neighborhood: "Bradbury Heights." It has a faded ribbon at the bottom, suggesting it was possibly related to some neighborhood event.

When Raymond and Dorothy were married back in 1934, Bradbury Heights would have been considered the outer suburbs, even though it was just over the district line, in Prince George's County, Maryland. The little one-story, four-room cottage they found on a gravel road named Mitchel Avenue, just a hundred yards from the district line, was perfect for a young couple, and affordable.

But when my sister, Nancy, came along in 1938, the little cottage seemed immediately cramped. Raymond and two of his friends, Romeo "Romie" Labona and a Mr. Futch, set about adding a second story to the house, complete with two street-facing dormer windows. On any given summer day, you could have found me sitting at the window, my crystal radio resting on the sill to get better reception.

To make way for the stairs to the second floor, the interior wall to Nancy's original bedroom was torn down, which doubled the size of the living room.

Climbing the stairs, you would first come upon an open landing that led to the door of Nancy's new room, which took up half of the upper floor. When I came along, the landing became my bedroom, which I eventually had to share with my younger brother, Kenny.

But Raymond wasn't done. If they were going to go to the trouble of adding a second story, why not go whole hog and expand the footprint of the house, adding a large kitchen with the latest 1940s appliances? And once that was done, why not dig a basement under the house, shovel by shovel? Raymond did all of that, and added a workshop and a pigeon coop to boot.

Let's join him and the family on the front steps of the remodeled house. When we look straight ahead, we see a street of many names. When Raymond and Dorothy moved in, the street was designated Mitchel Avenue, but as the years went by and the neighborhood's network of streets became more complex, the government decided that lettered streets was the way to go. Our street became R Street. But then the fire department decided that there were too many lettered streets. How could they possibly distinguish between our R Street and the R Street just over the line in the district? Well, smoke and flames might be a clue. On the other hand, maybe it was a good idea, so the firemen smiled when it became Rail Street, which is the designation it carries today.

Okay, let's look around a bit. Directly across the street is the home of Mr. and Mrs. Kite and their son, Eddy. Mrs.

Kite was the neighborhood's snoop and gossip. In the spring and summer, she would sit on her little front porch from dawn to dusk, keeping a sharp eye out for anything and everything. In the fall and winter, you could see her positioned at her front window, ever vigilant. She knew the comings and goings of everyone, and was more than willing to share what she saw. She was there to raise the alarm when Richard McWilliams threatened to stick me with a pitchfork when I was ten. And she was there when I was just a year old to see me tear off my diaper and race naked down the street to what I thought would be freedom, only to be scooped up from behind by my mother and spun in the air, thanks to the warning shouts of Mrs. Kite.

Now let's turn our heads to the left. Just beyond our tall white oak tree is the home of the Estes family, including girl-next-door crush Frances "Frankie" Estes, her brother Lenny, and her sister Bonnie.

Directly across the street from the Estes is the Harmon house, home to the girl who turned me down for the prom, Cookie Harmon. Back then, I thought she was so beautiful she must be a new species. If you had seen her promenading down R Street in her hot-pants, I think you would have agreed.

Okay, let's turn our attention away from the distraction of Cookie, and look to the right, where we'll see the home of the Purdy family, who were much better off than our family. Their home had a large, detached garage and a finished basement large enough to accommodate a pool table. We never had a conversation with them that was anything more than a reluctantly acknowledging grunt.

If we look farther down the street to the right, we'll see the home of the Griggs family. There's a brand new 1957 Chevy parked outside, making them the envy of every man on the street. Inside, we'll find Sweetie Griggs bouncing her two-year-old daughter, Becky, on her knee. Months later, Becky would be dead from brain cancer. The memory of the smallest coffin I've ever seen still sends chills up my spine.

Okay, we've looked every which way but backwards, so let's head to the backyard. There's one other house of importance just over the backyard fence. That home, a stately brick home almost twice as big as ours, is the home to a Greek-American family whose name escapes me. Their daughter, a beautiful Homecoming Queen, was badly disfigured in an auto accident, and spent her days mostly inside, away from the curious. When she did venture out, her face was always hidden behind a scarf or hood.

In memory, though, I think more about their fig tree than their daughter. On summer evenings, as I lay in bed, trying to go to sleep, I would count the figs as they fell from the tree, landed on the tin roof to my father's workshop, and rolled to the ground.

There's one other house of note. Just behind the Estes home is a vacant lot, and next to that is the home of one of my boyhood friends, Larry Dennison. Larry's father, an army veteran, was a wizard with wood. While many tried to forget the war and move on with their lives, Larry's father was in his workshop, making exact replicas of machine guns in wood. Larry and I would use them for battlefield re-creations in the vacant lot, using firecrackers as grenades.

It's been more than twenty years since I last set foot into the house that Raymond built. A Google search revealed that the home is still there, and Google even had a picture of the house, complete with a 360-degree view of it and the entire street. Our tall white oak tree is gone, as is the pigeon coop and Raymond's shop. The front door has been supplemented by a metal security gate, a far cry from the door we left unlocked and open most summer nights. The new owners have added a chain-link gate to the driveway, as well as a four-foot chain-link fence across the front of the property, which was always open to the street when we lived there. The size of the fence between our house and the Estes house, which was once a low, thin-wired fence that could easily be leaped, is now six feet tall. Tigers must live next door.

I manipulate the image to check out the rest of the street. The Estes house is still there, as well as the Harmon, Purdy, and Griggs homes. The home of Mrs. Kite is gone, replaced by a more modern home on the same small lot. I can't help thinking, though, that Mrs. Kite is still there, watching.

10
A DAY AT THE RACES

I reach into the box and pull out a silver-dollar size, stamped aluminum token, a promotional gimmick of a racetrack magazine called *The National Turf Digest*. Its motto: "Makes it Better for the Bettor." The token indicates that the magazine is just thirty-five cents at all leading newsstands.

I flip the coin over and am greeted by a message worthy of a snake-oil salesman: "WINNERS! Absolutely free from the dept. of L. DuPont French, America's Turf Wizard. Full particulars in magazine." Wow, maybe this magazine *is* worth thirty-five cents.

For whatever reason, Raymond keeps the coin and counts it among his treasures. It's a curiosity, and Raymond loves curiosities. I know he'd be the first person in line to see the bearded lady.

More to the point, the token reminds me of one of Raymond's passions: horse racing. Whenever he has money in his pocket, he loves nothing more than to head to any of a handful of racetracks in the Washington area, usually Laurel or Rosecroft. His hope is to parlay his meager cash into a fortune, and more often than not, he drags along the whole family to witness his almost guaranteed ascent to unimaginable wealth.

And that is what he has decided to do today, an announcement he makes as soon as we have safely deposited the customer's chair in his workshop. My mother was apparently in on the plot from the beginning. She has prepared a bag of butter-and-sugar sandwiches for us, so we can avoid the high-priced fare at the track.

I start to protest, but I can tell by the looks on my brother's and sister's faces that resistance is futile. "Plan 9 from Outer Space" will have to play out without me today. I join them on the customer's couch in the back of our Ford Econoline van, and off we go to the races.

Once there, my father buys a tout sheet or two from the local touts, who stand at the entrance, shouting out the worth of their information like carnival barkers. Words like *sure-fire winners, million-dollar nags*, and *ninety-seven percent accurate, all day, every day* are shouted at new arrivals.

Once he has his tout sheets, my father walks to the grandstand, where he will sit studying the sheets, his pencil poised above them to check off his selections, race by race. For the rest of the day, we will barely see him. Occasionally, we'll spot him along the rail, shouting obscenities at the losing jockeys. Other times, he'll be near the paddock, studying the horses every move as they're saddled up and brought out to the track.

More famously, however, we'll see him running to the betting window, absolutely certain of his selection. "It's the two horse!"

When Raymond returns, we join him at the rail to see this certainty unfold. And it does! The two horse wins!

Unfortunately, my father didn't bet on the two horse. As he always did, he changes his mind at the window, switching to a different horse.

"I just had a hunch," he says, ripping up the ticket and tossing the pieces in the air. Then he pulls out his tout sheets and pencil and disappears into the crowd to predict the next winner, leaving the rest of us standing there, munching on the sweet grittiness of the butter-and-sugar sandwiches and watching the crowd of winners and losers.

My favorite thing to do at the track is search through the losing tickets that litter the ground, looking for fifty-dollar tickets. By the end of the day, I have a whole deck of them, enough lost money to buy a Cadillac. On the ride home, I share them with Raymond.

"Well, at least you didn't lose *this* much, dad."

Everyone laughs except Raymond. The customer's deposit is now completely gone, and all Raymond has to show for it is a couple of pies, which is all the profit he'll see from reupholstering the sofa and chair. Looks like another night of beans on Wonder Bread for dinner. And some bitter-sweet pie. So it goes.

11
ATTACK OF THE TACK

I reach into Raymond's treasure box once more and am met with a surprise, a *painful* surprise. I pull my hand out much faster than it went in, complete with an upholstery tack stuck on the tip of my index finger.

I have to shake my head. *Of course* there would be a tack in his treasure box, even if he hadn't intended there to be one. It's hard to imagine how many hundreds of thousands of tacks my father dealt with in his life, but they were everywhere, most notably on his shoes. As he worked, he would drop tacks to the floor. And then he'd step on them. And then the whole process would be repeated again and again until the soles of his shoes were mostly upholstery tacks.

When he came into the house, as he was doing now, the late afternoon following the fiasco at the racetrack, he sounded like a slow-moving tap dancer as he moved through the kitchen, looking for me.

"Lenny, I need you."

Alerted by the sound of his shoes, I have already retreated from the kitchen and made my way through the dining room and the living room, and halfway up the stairs to the bedroom I share with my brother, Kenny.

Raymond calls again. There is no anger in his voice, so I decide to take a chance and let him find me.

He spots me on the stairs. "Ah, there you are. Come on and give me a hand with that sofa. I want to open her up and see what we got."

I know immediately what he's referring to, and it makes perfect sense considering how poorly he did at the racetrack. He's going to open up the sofa to see what's inside.

Perhaps treasure.

Moments later, we are in his backyard workshop, the customer's sofa sitting on a pair of sawhorses, ready for gutting. My job is to help him tilt the sofa up a bit, so it just rests on two legs, one on either sawhorse. While I hold the sofa in that angled position, he takes a razor blade, slides it through the fabric at the sofa's base, and drags it the full length of the sofa. Things begin falling out.

Treasure!

When English archaeologist Howard Carter opened the tomb of Tutankhamun, he saw "things, wonderful things" that would give the world insight into the life of the young pharaoh and his world. So too was every "opening" Raymond made to each and every piece of furniture that made its way through his workshop. We were not just seeing wonderful things, we were furniture archaeologists, actually peeking into the lives of our customers, their world encapsulated in what they had allowed to become entombed in the creases of their couch.

Today, there is the usual assortment of foodstuffs, mostly flattened popcorn, plus a few cashews, a sure sign of wealth. No peanuts for her. No, sir, just the finest cashews. And another telltale sign of wealth: fancy toothpicks, the kind with colorful cellophane tassels, dropped casually into a crack in the sofa when the hostess wasn't looking. No doubt it once speared a delectable, multilayered hors d'oeuvre.

My father flicks all of this aside. He's interested in money and jewelry, and the sofa doesn't disappoint. Along with $2.37 in change, there is a crumpled five-dollar bill, a couple of French francs, a single faux pearl earring, and one final item that evokes a long, slow whistle from my father: a diamond ring.

Let me pause here briefly to lay down the rules, namely Raymond's Rules of Salvage.

Rule One: Anything found in a customer's piece of furniture, by rights, belongs to the finder.

Rule Two: The "anything" referred to in Rule One does not include items of great value, which must be returned to the customer when the item of furniture is returned.

Rule Three: From time to time, on a case-by-case basis, the finder may ignore Rule Two.

I can tell my father is struggling with Rule Three. The diamond is as big as a kernel of corn, and the gold is 24 carat. It could fetch enough money to buy a real delivery truck, or help him pay down his debt to the fabric store, Bedelle's. Or maybe we could buy a new washing machine, buy some decent furniture for our living room, fix the bathroom, or—hey, here's an idea—buy me a bicycle.

The more I think of this, of course, the more I'm persuaded that the found wealth would just send him off to the racetrack to sort out the nags from the champions, and we'd be right back where we started.

Raymond seems to be considering all of this, with the possible exception of the bicycle, but then he puffs out his cheeks and shakes his head. He has decided that Rule Two applies.

"We'll give these back to her. She must have been sick at losing them."

He pockets the ring and the earring, then turns back to the money. "This, on the other hand, is ours by rights. What do you think we should do with it?"

I already know where his mind is going, so I help him along. "Dixie Pig!"

There will be no beans and bread tonight. Tonight, we will have barbecued beef, pork, and chicken, with sides of coleslaw and potato salad. The restaurant is two miles away, but it is well worth the walk.

My father hands me the five-dollar bill. "Go get 'em."

I do. Oh, I do.

12
THEY'RE DROPPING BUMS ON GERMANY!

I reach back into Raymond's treasure box and pull out an item that immediately gives me chills, and concerns. It's a golden coin, about the size of a fifty-cent piece. One side pronounces, "1833-1933 SOUVENIR: A Century of Progress, Chicago." Okay, no cause for alarm there. But the other side . . .

Oh, the other side.

On the other side is a large swastika, the dreaded hooked cross. Oh, my god, was my father a closet Nazi? No, no he wasn't. The wording around the rim of the coin makes me think otherwise: "Membership Emblem of the Don't Worry Club, GOOD LUCK."

After some research, I determine that prior to the Nazi's coopting of the swastika, it was a universal symbol of good luck. First used in Eurasia nearly 7,000 years ago, it is still in use as a sacred symbol in Hinduism, Buddhism, Jainism, and Odinism. The symbol also has a long history in Europe. The Nazis thought it represented their ancestors, their Aryan identity, and by artful racist twisting, their rightful destiny.

The word swastika is derived from the Sanskrit svastika, meaning "good fortune." And, as shown on this coin, each hook of the cross contains secondary symbols of luck: a wishbone, a horseshoe, a four-leaf clover, and even three Egyptian hieroglyphs representing good fortune and auspiciousness. It was common for businesses to hand these out as promotional items, even into the 1930s.

My father never traveled more than a few hundred miles from Washington, D.C., and was never in Chicago, so I assume the coin was salvaged from a customer's chair as a chilling curiosity. I can imagine my father, a man of great superstition, carrying this coin in his front pocket, to give him luck in pigeon racing and at the racetrack.

The coin also brings back a memory.

I'm in the dining room, doing homework, while my father is in the living room, watching television on our eight-inch Admiral black-and-white television. I was never a big fan of homework. My goal was to race through it as quickly as I could, so I could turn my attention to another teacher: our television.

The image on our television is not just eight inches, though; it is actually an astounding eleven inches thanks to a big magnifying glass attached to the front of the screen, a common accessory back in the day. That amazing image is the reason our neighbors come by most nights to watch television with us. In fact, all the other dining room chairs are in the living room, lined up and waiting for our neighbors.

There's a program on, a documentary of some sort. I try not to pay attention. I'm focused on a math problem involving two trains, one headed to Washington from

Baltimore at thirty miles an hour, the other headed to Baltimore from Washington at forty miles an hour. The question: at what point will the trains pass each other? I really don't care, I just want to get through the problem, so I can join my father and watch some TV.

And then my father starts shouting. "Come and see, they're dropping bums on Germany."

My trains collide at an unknown location as I struggle to make sense of what he is saying. Why would anyone drop bums on anyone, even Germany? It would be both impractical and cruel. With visions of armed men rounding up bums off the street and forcing them into bombers, I drop my pencil and dash to the living room, just in time to see bombers unloading their bombs on Germany.

My father, it seems, has trouble pronouncing certain words. When he's thinking *bombs*, he's actually saying *bums*. I sit down in a chair and watch the devastation as my father makes explosion noises. "Ka-boom, ka-boom!"

I glance back into the dining room. Rescue workers are on the scene of the train wreck, searching for survivors. They seem to have the situation well in hand, so I decide to stay where I am. Sid Caesar should be on any minute now.

I wonder if Sid's ever thought of a comedy sketch involving bums over Germany.

13
ALL THAT FLOATS

I start to reach into Raymond's treasure box again, but the pain in my tack-attacked finger brings back a stream of memories.

Oh, those tacks. Not only did they adorn Raymond's shoes, turning him into a Frankenstein monster of sorts, but they surely lined his entire gastrointestinal system. Back then, long before the staple gun would replace hammer and tack, every upholsterer had their own technique for tacking. You could pick up a tack with your hand, place it where you want it to go in, and then drive it home with your upholstery hammer, a thin-headed tool designed specifically for driving tacks.

That works, of course, but it's slow and tedious, and hard on the fingers. Those tacks, as I am well aware, have very sharp points. So my father's solution, if you can call it that, was to pour a handful of tacks into his mouth, and then withdraw them one by one with the magnetic tip of his hammer. I was always happy to see him do this, because it meant any thought of a verbal attack against me was off the table. The most that I could expect was a spray of nails spit in my direction.

Anyway, as he went along, deftly extracting, aiming, and driving the tacks into his target chair or sofa, he would occasionally feel the need to swallow. If he was quick enough, he could spit the tacks back into his hand, swallow, and return the tacks to his mouth. On the other hand, if his gag reflex took hold, he would literally be spitting nails around his workshop. Some, no doubt, made their way down his throat. I've often wondered whether the ingestion of tacks had anything to do with his ultimate death. Then again, maybe the ingestion of iron helped him live longer.

At any rate, Raymond's hammer itself brings back more memories.

Raymond was an alarmist, a man who would often overreact when the proper response was to stay calm. I remember a day when I was about ten and the family had gone to one of my father's favorite fishing spots, Allen's Fresh, which was usually packed with picnicking families and fishermen every weekend. We were there to do both, although I know my mother and older sister had come along reluctantly, because besides fishing, there was little to do.

So as they prepared the picnic, my younger brother and I trudged along behind my father to find just the right spot to fish, which involved walking through sucking mud and closely spaced saplings, and around scores of fishermen, all urging us with gestures and whispered shouts to be quiet so as not to scare off the fish.

About half an hour later, as we sat bored to death for lack of any fish, my father heard a splash. Could have been a fish jumping out of the water. Or a frog. Or a rock thrown by a child. But my father leaped to the most dramatic possibility: someone had fallen into the water and was right that moment sinking under the surface, drowning for lack of help. And not just anyone. I'm sure he pictured a homeless, orphaned little girl who hadn't eaten in days, perhaps weeks, a sweet little thing, perhaps named Little Nell, who had perhaps strayed too close to the water's edge, swooned from hunger, and fell into the raging calm waters.

Raymond immediately threw down his fishing rod and began racing through the saplings, passing stunned fisherman after stunned fisherman, screaming his head off for someone to for god's sake help the poor child that was drowning. My brother and I trailed behind, trying our best to avoid the stares of the fishermen.

And, of course, it turned out to be nothing. There was no sweet Little Nell.

So, a year later, as I sat in our kitchen, eating my classic breakfast of Pepsi and a donut, I was not in the least alarmed to see my father rush from his backyard shop, looking like the devil himself was chasing him.

He burst into the kitchen, shouting for my mother. "Dickie, Dickie!" His choice of pet names clearly indicated that he was either sick or frightened, which were the only two occasions he ever used that name for her. His other pet name for her, Nuisance, was reserved for times when he was angry with her.

My mother looked up calmly from behind her sewing machine, not the least bit concerned and said, "What?"

My father, clearly shaken, could only stammer. "The-the-the-hammer . . . *floated!*"

After my mother calmed him down, he explained that while he was working on a sofa, one of his hammers had floated up off the workbench and then disappeared. My mother was incredulous, as was I, so the two of us traipsed out to the workshop, finding nothing out of the ordinary, except that there was no hammer on the workbench, which didn't mean much. Even so, the "floating hammer" story became a staple of my father's, and he would recount it again and again over the years, whenever the subject of ghosts came up. "Remember that floating hammer?"

Now we have to fast-forward many years, to 1992, as my father lay dying in his hospital bed, the family gathered round him, waiting for the end. He went from face to face, acknowledging us, and then squinted, looking away from us to the corner of the room, his last words:

"Why does the angel have my hammer?"

In the annals of final words, those must stand out. Although my mom was not to be outdone. Her last words, four years later, were: "I really want to have sex!"

You go, Mom!

14
READY BOILER ONE

Raymond was shaped by many things, and certainly deaths played a large role in his life view. The deaths of his sister and his young playmate Darla had been traumatic, but nothing like the devastation he felt after his friend and coworker had plummeted down an elevator shaft right before his eyes, changing Raymond's life—and mine—forever.

But there is another death we should talk about, and that is the death of Raymond's father, Frank. Mean-spirited and abusive, he was an outright drunk who grew meaner still when he was in his cups, which was almost always. His anger was mostly directed at Raymond's mother, Daisey Bell, but he was also known to take a strap to any of his twelve children when the mood suited him. I'm sure that's why Raymond never took a strap or belt to me or Kenny, although he always threatened to do so.

The boys in the family—Raymond, Stanley, George, and Fred—when they grew older, would gang up on their father to keep him from seriously injuring Daisey, who seemed to take all of the drunken rage in stride. Of all the boys, only Fred would take up the drink. The others remained teetotalers and nonsmokers their entire lives.

My grandmother, a diminutive woman barely five-feet tall, tolerated the abuse and seventeen pregnancies, and lived to the century-pushing old age of ninety-nine. Frank faced a different fate entirely.

Frank worked at a manufacturing plant as a boiler repairman. If anything went wrong with the boiler, Frank was the man who had to fix things, quickly. Profit was on the line, and safety was never a thought.

On one fine summer evening when Frank was forty-six, a messenger arrived at his Southwest Washington home, with an urgent message to come at once to the factory. The boiler had broken down, and it had to be repaired before the morning shift, or else. "Or else" meant his job was on the line.

Frank, already half in his cups, gave the messenger a nod, staggered out of the house, and followed the messenger back to the plant. It seems that something had gone wrong with a steam control valve within the outer container of the boiler. Left as is, the boiler would have surely exploded when its automatic start-up sequence began. Fixing it would require Frank to suck in his beer belly, crawl through a small round portal on the side of the boiler, and make the repair in the boiler's steam chamber.

It was not a technically difficult fix, but the job would take a couple of hours. Frank grabbed his tools and a replacement valve, and dutifully climbed into the boiler chamber. Even though the boiler was offline, the residual heat was intense. Coworkers had to keep feeding cups of water to Frank as he worked. Minutes ticked away to hours as he struggled to replace the valve.

Finally, the repair was done and Frank gathered up his tools and the faulty valve and began to climb out through the portal.

But he couldn't get back out.

The heat and the water had made him swell up enough to prevent him from squeezing back out through the portal. He tried and tried again, coworkers tugging on his arms in a race against the clock. The boiler would restart automatically at dawn, and there was no handy failsafe switch to stop the process.

Workers jumped on a company truck and raced to a nearby icehouse to fetch several hundred pounds of ice. Their thought was to cool Frank down enough to reduce the swelling that was preventing his exit.

It didn't work.

At dawn, right on schedule, the boiler kicked in, roasting my grandfather alive. When the boiler shut down automatically ten hours later, workers were able to climb in and retrieve his body. Even then, he was too bloated to make it through the small portal. Saws were brought in and he was dismembered.

Raymond never told me this story directly. It is a story he had only shared with my mother, in the small hours, when the house was quiet and still.

15
PIGEON MAN

The flight has taken more than eight hours, and it has been harrowing: rain, strong headwinds, and the buffeting that comes from wind shear and turbulence. But I can see the rooftops of the homes in my neighborhood as I descend and land. I know what to expect next. That man who takes care of me will grab me from behind, rip off the rubber ring on my left leg, and run it through his damned clock. But at least I'm home now, safe in the wings of my mate, with stories to tell about a bad run-in with a pigeon hawk.

Raymond was a pigeon man, so it is no surprise to find a pigeon band in his treasure box. And I can guess that it is the band worn by his best pigeon, Rocky, who tallied several wins, including a first place in a 500-miler. The trophy for that win would have joined about twenty others on a bookshelf my father kept in the corner of the living room at the foot of the staircase, probably the only thing ever dusted in our house with any frequency.

Pigeon racing was my father's passion. He'd started as a teenager, way back in the 1920s, and the first thing he built when he and my mother moved into their little one-bedroom cottage in Bradbury Heights was a pigeon coop.

Although he wasn't a carpenter, he did have some skills with a hammer and saw. In the coming years, he and his best friend and fellow pigeon racer, Romeo "Romie" Labona, would build his workshop and add a second floor to the house to accommodate me, my older sister, and my younger brother, Kenny.

The pigeon coop—or as I referred to it, the poop coop, because I was the one tasked to clean it—was built to look like the house, a simple white clapboard building with Plain Jane trim and a green-shingled roof. In its heyday, the coop held more than a hundred birds, more or less, depending on our financial situation. If there were too many birds to feed, Raymond would thin the flock by killing, plucking, and frying up the young squabs, which he assured us tasted "just like chicken." I can still see them sizzling in the frying pan, Raymond poking at them with a fork, a memory that still makes me cringe.

One of my mother's main complaints about the birds was my father's birds-come-first approach to feeding the family. Pigeon feed came before bread. That's just how it was. On the other hand, the money seemed well spent. Pigeon racing calmed him, centered him, and gave him a quiet place to retreat. In times of stress, he would go to the coop, release the birds, and watch them circle the house and the neighborhood. One of my mother's favorite tacks to calm any situation, including outbursts at me or my brother, was to tell him to "go outside and feed the birds." He would always take a step back, give her a nod, and head for the coop.

Feeding the birds, of course, inevitably led to pigeon poop, which led to the need for cleaning the coop, which led to me scraping up buckets of poop and spreading it around the backyard, particularly in our little victory garden. Thanks to the pigeon poop, our little garden produced tomatoes as big as cantaloupes and zucchini of monstrous proportions. I could be wrong, but I'm pretty sure the only way Jack and the Beanstalk works is with a good dose of pigeon poop.

In addition to cleaning the coop, I would also ride shotgun on Raymond's pigeon-training trips. The process was simple. First select the birds you want to race. Then take them on successive trips farther and farther away from the coop. The first trip might be just a mile, but some of the training runs would reach 200 miles or more. Back then, in the late 1950s, getting 200 miles away from Washington, D.C. wasn't easy. The Washington Beltway was still years away, so getting to Virginia from Maryland meant going through Washington. And once in Virginia, most if not all the roads were little two-lane, asphalt affairs, many without center stripes. It was an adventure to say the least.

Adventure—seeing something new, *anything* new— was probably the only reason I went along, because spending hours alone in a car with my father was not my idea of fun. The rides were mostly spent in silence, the only sound the cooing of the pigeons from the crates of birds crammed into the backseat of our 1950 Plymouth. Our conversations, when we had them, centered on the needs for food, gas, or bathroom breaks. That was it. I knew from experience never to ask, "Are we there yet?"

When we did get there, usually with two crates of birds, we tried our best to simulate how the birds would be released during a race. The gentleman tasked with that job was called The Liberator, who would always be accompanied by at least one other man to assure that the liberator did his job as required. The idea was to quickly release the birds, so none had an advantage.

My father would open one crate, and I'd open the other, on signal, and we'd watch the birds for a few minutes as they circled, found their bearings, and headed back home. Not all of them made it back. Some decided to live out the rest of their lives where they were released. Others decided that a good city park was a fine place to live. Still others fell victim to pigeon hawks. But most made it back home.

My mother's job was to do her best in identifying the first birds back. What my father called his "money birds." Once the birds were released, he'd give her a phone call and tell her when to expect the first birds. My mother hated doing this, because she really couldn't tell the difference between a "chocolate" and a "blue-checked hen."

Arguments ensued, of course.

"So, who came back first?" my father would say.

My mother would hesitate, her voice rising. "A blue one?"

"And when did it arrive?"

"Um, about three-*ish*."

My father would groan in frustration and stalk off to the pigeon coop to see which birds actually made it back.

Once the birds were sufficiently trained, Raymond would enter them into races sponsored by his pigeon club. The day before a race, he would take his pigeon clock and the birds he wanted to race to the clubhouse. There, each bird would be banded with a rubber ring on their left leg. Raymond's clock, along with the clocks of the other members, would be synchronized and then sealed with a metal wire and lead seal to prevent tampering during the race.

His birds would be added to one of a dozen or more crates under the supervision of The Liberator, who would load them into his truck, drive them to the designated release point, and let them fly.

Then the wait began. Once Raymond received a call from the club telling him the time of the release, he would sit down with a pencil and paper and calculate when he might expect the first birds to arrive. And once he knew that time, there would be a family meeting.

"The first bird should arrive at about two, so no one goes into the backyard after 1:30," he would say.

And then he'd turn to me. "And no slamming doors."

And then he'd turn to my sister, Nancy. "And no playing Elvis."

And then he'd turn to my brother, Kenny. "And keep those friends of yours away. Or better yet, go to their house."

And then he'd turn to my mother. "Make sure all this happens."

And then he'd turn on his heels and head to his workshop to work on a customer's chair or sofa. Then, at about 1:30, he'd go outside and sit in a chair along the side of the house, waiting for his birds.

The hope was that once a bird arrived, it would land on the landing board and immediately head into the pigeon coop through a small controlled opening at the end of the landing board. Raymond would then grab the bird, remove its rubber ring, and crank the ring into the clock, which would record on a paper spool the exact time the bird had arrived. Usually, though, the process involved a lot of coaxing from my father as he attempted to corral the bird by making cooing sounds and waving his arms. Sometimes this worked beautifully, but other times it could take minutes, valuable minutes, before the bird complied.

The process would continue, bird after bird, until all the birds came back or my father was sure they were well out of the race, or just plain gone. He would then take the clock and his hopes and dreams to the clubhouse to see who had won the race, including a fine trophy and one or more racing pools.

Who actually won was always a contentious affair, because math was involved, and everyone in the club seemed skeptical of math. Racing before the GPS era was both simple and complicated. When you joined a racing club, the first order of business was to have your coop professionally surveyed to determine its exact longitude and latitude.

Then, once you'd turned over your clock to the judge, the judge would unseal it and pull out the paper record of the bird's arrival time. He would then calculate the speed of the bird as it traveled X distance from coordinates Y,Z to coordinates A,B. Then he'd repeat that process for every clock delivered to the club. The fastest bird won.

But again, math was involved, so results were checked, challenged, rechecked, challenged, and rechecked again and again until everyone was satisfied. But it was usually the case that no one was satisfied. The losers thought they'd been robbed, and the winner didn't have the satisfaction of a clear victory.

So it was not unusual for my father to arrive home with a trophy, a handful of cash, and a black eye.

"You should see the other guy."

16
FRIENDSHIP

The next item out of the box is a gold men's "buckle ring," a ring designed to look like a buckled belt, and meant to symbolize love or friendship. The theme: we go together like a belt and buckle.

Giving such rings was very popular in the Victorian era, and the rings are available even today. The question is why is this ring in Raymond's treasure box? Who gave it? Who received it? Did it belong to my father? Or did he find it in a customer's sofa?

It's hard to know. I have no memory of my father wearing any ring other than his simple wedding band. It may be that my mother gave it to him before they were married, and he set it aside after the marriage, the wedding band superseding the friendship ring. On the other hand, at age 17, my mother would have never had the resources to buy a gold ring.

It seems likely that my father retrieved it from a piece of furniture and immediately invoked Rule Three of Raymond's Rules of Salvage, never returning it.

There are a couple of things I find interesting about the ring. First, it can be worn with the end of the belt pointing either to the right or to the left. Would there have been any significance to that? Would switching it back and forth be a signal of some kind between the two friends or lovers? I just don't know.

Second, the ring fits me, which is spooky. Was the ring intended for me all along? No, that's just silly. But it does bring back memories of one of my father's friendships.

If Raymond ever had a true bromance, it would have been with his friend Romeo "Romie" Labona. There was a certain Mutt and Jeff feeling to their friendship. My father was just under six feet tall, but Romie was nearly a foot shorter, with a prominent belly and thick, muscular arms. My father's eyes were blue, and Romie's were brown. If they shared any physical attribute it would have been their jet-black hair, although Romie's doo was more severe, a combed-back affair that looked like a hair helmet.

Romie belonged to the same pigeon club, so they shared interests. And he was an ace auto mechanic, which meant my father could get repairs for the cost of parts alone. Throughout the years, Romie repaired our 1950 Plymouth, our Chevrolet station wagon, and most notably, our Ford Econoline van, the only vehicle my father ever bought "sort of new."

The van was from the first model year, and it came with a bushel of lemons. Everything that could break down did break down. Fortunately, Romie was always there.

"What's it this time, Ray, black smoke, white smoke— blue, gray?"

Any answer meant trouble. Blue smoke: burning oil, indicating bad engine seals or worn-out piston rings. Gray smoke: Maybe the same problem, burning oil, or perhaps transmission fluid being burned in the engine due to a faulty vacuum modulator. White smoke: could be just condensation burning off in the exhaust system, or if the smoke is thicker, it could be the "cheery" sign of a blown head gasket, a damaged cylinder head, or a cracked engine block—um, no thanks to that. Black smoke: the engine is burning too much fuel, which could mean a clogged fuel line or faulty fuel flow, maybe from a bad fuel-pressure regulator.

Raymond would usually shrug at the question. "Dunno, maybe all of them?"

"Jesus, Ray," Romie would say. "Turn on the damn engine and let me have a look-see."

Romie would go to the back of the van and watch the smoke coming out, interpreting the results as if he were parsing a message from an Indian smoke signal. Then, without a word to my father, he would grunt and head for his own car to retrieve his tools. Sometimes he'd give me a wink or a nod as a signal for me to follow him. He'd pop open his trunk and begin pointing at the tools he wanted me to carry.

Once back at the car, he'd give my father the diagnosis. "Something in the fuel system. Go have some lemonade. This will take a while."

Romie would then set to work, one hour leading to two, and sometimes on and on until the lightning bugs came out, my mother supplying sandwiches and lemonade, as required. Most times, the fix would work, at little cost, but there would be other times when only the color of the smoke changed.

This happened so frequently, I can still see Romie standing at the back of the van, shaking his head, and offering a new diagnosis. "Aw, shit."

17
THE SECOND SON

The next item out of the box, my younger brother's military dog tags, unleashes a stream of emotions I can barely contain. My brother was wonderful and terrible, kind and violent, and seemingly possessed by demons he could never control.

It's curious that Raymond has included the dog tags among his treasures, because he never expressed pride in my brother, or me, during his life. We were never hugged, never given an "attaboy" slap on the back, and never offered a single word of praise or encouragement. He never attended our baseball games or soccer matches, so homeruns and goals went unacknowledged. We were "no account bastards" when rage would overpower him and he began screaming at us no more than an inch from our faces. Like some drill sergeant. But just imagine a drill sergeant getting in your face beginning at age two and never stopping until you took your escape route to college.

My mother was there to defend us, of course. When Raymond set into me or my brother, or both of us, she would separate us as quickly as she could, sending Raymond back to his workshop or pigeon coop and us to our room. Then, when things had calmed down, she would come upstairs to our room to console us. "He doesn't mean it" was her usual defense, but it always rang hollow. The truth was he was emotionally disturbed and there was nothing to be done about it.

In many ways, Raymond just lurked around our lives, emotionally distant, there but not there, appearing only to vent his anger and frustration at us. When someone gets within an inch of your face and screams at you, you have many options. I chose to not react at all on the outside—not give him the satisfaction of victory. But on the inside, I was withdrawing from the world, isolating myself, curling myself into a ball of suppressed anger.

My brother Kenny's reaction was different; he screamed back and stormed away, matching obscenity with obscenity as he raced up the stairs to our room. But he was hurt deeply as well. I'm not sure why he turned to alcohol at the age of twelve. It could have been his response to Raymond's emotional abuse, or it could have been some genetic trigger provided by our alcoholic grandfather, Frank.

Whatever the reason, alcohol controlled him the rest of his life, even during his brief career in the U.S. Air Force. After basic training, he was assigned to a base in North Africa, as a military policeman. One night, as he stood guard, he thought he saw an intruder climbing the perimeter fence. He shot him down.

The problem was my brother was drunk at the time, and the man he shot was just a passerby. Kenny was summarily discharged in short order and sent back home, where he remained for another thirty years, until my mother died.

My sister, Nancy, and I transferred our share of the meager inheritance to Kenny, letting him sell the house and move into a trailer, with a small cushion of cash, enough to carry him while he searched, at age 50, for the first steady job in his life.

He eventually found a job as a clerk at a nearby auto parts store, and seemed to be doing well. But then one afternoon a few months later, as I sat at a conference table during a staff retreat in Florida, a colleague tapped me on the shoulder and quietly beckoned me out of the room.

"I'm afraid I have bad news," he said. "Your brother has died."

I don't recall exactly what I said next, but at some point I told my colleague that I was "shocked but not surprised." My brother lived life with his foot on the gas pedal, and could never seem to find the brake.

Kenny died of an apparent heart attack while sleeping in the arms of his lover, a drug addict who would die of cancer just weeks later. There is some question about when the lover realized that Kenny was dead. She was strung out on drugs, so it is very possible that Kenny had been dead for more than a day when she realized he was not responding to her voice.

What we were told by the funeral director, however, was that the ambulance driver had apparently left Kenny's body in the ambulance outside the morgue overnight.

In any event, his body was so badly decomposed, there was never a thought of an open casket. At the funeral, two men came up to me and introduced themselves as "house guests" of my brother. They, too, were alcoholics, and went on and on about Kenny's kindness and generosity, but both seemed reluctant to provide any details about Kenny's death.

"We were drunk, you see," said one.

The other one scoffed. "Well, you was drunk, sure, but not me."

"No, we was *both* drunk," said the first one. "I know drunk when I see it, you idiot."

The other one ignored the comment and turned back to me. "Drunk or no, there was nothing to be done. When we heard her screams, we ran in, lickety-split, but your poor brother was gone."

"Gone he was," said the first one. "And yes, 'tweren't nothin' to be done."

The funeral was lightly attended, which meant that only I and the house guests were available as pall bearers. We managed to drop the coffin twice before the grave-digging crew came to our aid.

The house guests and Kenny's lover disappeared the next day, after stripping the trailer of anything worth selling, including Raymond's trophies.

Kenneth S. Boswell, 1946-2000. Rest in peace, my brother.

18
FRAYED, NOT SHAKEN

The next item out of Raymond's treasure box, what was once an ornate convention badge, is in the last stages of disintegration. The red, white, and blue ribbon under the small brass nameplate has unraveled to single threads, barely able to support the crossed brass swords they once supported grandly.

It's clearly my father's badge; "R. Boswell" inked on the paper within the brass rectangle makes it a certainty. But what the badge was for is a mystery. The crossed swords, reminiscent of the swords you'd find on a Union soldier's cap, suggest some sort of patriotic theme or group, as does the colorful ribbon.

But Raymond was never in the military, and as far as I know, didn't belong to any groups that would suggest a badge so clearly patriotic. My best guess is that the name tag was handed out to members of Raymond's pigeon club at their annual Fourth of July bash.

I only attended one of these, but it was much more than I would have expected from a pigeon club. There was food, of course, and a pay-as-you-get-drunk bar, but there was also an accordion player who roamed around, playing requests as he cruised among the tables draped with bunting. There was even a country singer who was making a name for himself on a local TV show: Jimmy Dean. He would go on to fame and a sausage empire, but at this event, he followed the accordion player's lead, singing and strumming as he walked around the room.

Everyone was having a wonderful time, except kids like me who couldn't abide country music or accordions. As I looked around the room, I saw a lot of cringing and wincing from children being confronted by the musicians. Some even got up from their seats and ran to the safety of the farthest corner.

But back to the convention badge. The swords are in their scabbards, and each scabbard has a brass loop on its tip to hang yet another badge. These would have been used to add badges denoting which among the members was president, treasurer, liberator, and so on.

My father would have never accepted any position of leadership. He could have done well, I think, because he had an outgoing personality, particularly in group situations, but he preferred the life of a loner. He already had responsibility for a wife and three children, and worked ten hours a day. Added responsibility, even if it came with the perquisites of leadership, was never on his agenda.

I turn back to the frayed ribbon and try, unsuccessfully, to nudge the threads back into a single piece. It's as hopeless as the furniture in our house. As you might imagine, a man who spends all day working on the furniture of customers has little interest in spending even a minute reupholstering his own.

As a result, our house looked like a collection of furniture selected from the deep-discount section of

Goodwill. And it may as well have been. Frayed arms, pee stains, food stains, collapsed springs that made sitting uncomfortable, and a host of other furniture maladies were the norm for our furniture.

Occasionally, customers who balked at the cost of reupholstering would offer Raymond the sofa or chair, either free or for a modest price. Most were not even interested in having their furniture reupholstered; they just wanted someone to come to their house and cart the damned thing away. In most cases, my father would oblige, unless carting it away involved multiple staircases.

If the item of furniture was in better condition than the furniture in our living room, it would become our "new" furniture. The result was an eclectic assortment of furniture of various periods and styles, a 1950s-modern sofa sitting beside a Louis XVI chair, the sofa looking like it had barely survived a direct hit from an atom bomb, the chair looking less grand than the grandeur of Versailles. It looked more like a Louis I chair that had been attacked by cats.

And forget about color coordination. The furniture was any color that came through the door. I think a designer would have had three choices: faint, run, or throw up. And perhaps they would have found a way to do all three.

Sometimes Raymond would come home with replacement furniture that was over the top in ugliness. I remember one particular sofa that had our whole family begging him not to bring it in the house. It was shaped like a boomerang, and was the color of chartreuse gone rancid.

Despite our protests, it would serve as the family's couch for more than a decade before being replaced by a sofa given to him by a woman with sixteen cats.

I'll leave that to your imagination.

19
IT'S JUST BUSINESS

The small aluminum token is about the size of a nickel, has a small hole at its center, and includes the same message on both sides: "Tax Commission, Sales Tax Token, State of Washington."

A quick visit to Wikipedia gives me a little more information: "Sales tax tokens were fractional cent devices used to pay sales tax on very small purchases in many American states during the years of the Great Depression. Tax tokens were created as a means for consumers to avoid being 'overcharged' by having to pay a full penny tax on purchases of 5 or 10 cents. Issued by private firms, by municipalities, and by twelve state governments, sales tax tokens were generally issued in multiples of 1 mill (1/10 cent)."

The token is clearly a find from my father's many furniture salvage operations—Raymond had never been to the state of Washington. It's another curiosity for the treasure box. At the same time, it brings back two memories of Raymond's business acumen.

As a self-employed businessman, Raymond had to rely on his own skills and those of my mother to handle financial transactions and recordkeeping for the company.

I use the word *company* loosely, because he was never incorporated, and tried his best to fly under the radar where income tax was concerned. Way under the radar.

My mother served as accountant, recording sales and expenses in a little ledger book she bought at the Ben Franklin Five and Dime. Whether she was scrupulous in accurately recording every financial transaction is open to question. My father preferred cash from customers, which opened the door to hidden income. And we were living on the lowest tier of the middle class—struggling but not starving—so the door may have been wide open.

Raymond's customer invoices were hand-written on a simple notepad. He'd write down all the particulars, for example, "Sofa, $90," and then he'd pick up his business stamp, which consisted of his name and the image of a sofa, press it firmly into a black-ink pad, and then stamp it down on the paper. That was it. No duplicate copies for the record books. The only official record of the transaction would be in the ledger book, if it ever made it there.

Fortunately, the IRS never came calling for an audit of the books. Unfortunately, the state of Maryland came after them for evading state sales tax. Virginia and the District of Columbia could have, but didn't. The result was devastating to a family that was already living hand to mouth most days. That extra payment to the state each month for the next seven years meant an immediate curtailment of "discretionary" expenses like clothes and food.

The timing couldn't have been worse. When I was twelve, I was five feet, two inches tall. When I was thirteen, I was six feet, one inch tall. I was skinny, so my growth had little to do with the size of my shirts, although they grew tight enough to pop buttons now and then. My pants were another story. Until I was personally able to save up enough money—mowing lawns, raking leaves, sweeping porches and sidewalks, collecting soda bottles, and so on—I was forced to wear the pants I had. The cuffs of my pants were at least six inches from the top of my shoes, making me look like I was wearing clam diggers, which tickled my friends so much they nicknamed me "Tall Toes."

The problem with clothing persisted right up until I was dropped off by Raymond and my mom at the University of Maryland for my freshman year. Raymond handed me a two dollar bill for expenses, and my mother handed me a small shopping bag containing the unwashed sheets from my bed. I was already wearing all the clothes I owned, including a too-tight shirt, too-short pants, and tennis shoes held together by white medical tape. Those shoes would see me through the coming winter with the help of plastic grocery bags taped around them.

But enough about me.

Raymond, as I have said, was a loner. Because of his "nervous breakdown," he didn't want anything to do with a regular job. And despite our family's financial struggles, he saw no reason to change his business methods. He could have advertised, but he didn't. That would cost money. Word-of-mouth praise for the quality of his work was how he got new business. He could have increased prices, but he was afraid customers would balk and word-of-mouth would go south. Affordable prices and volume were his mantra.

Not that there weren't temptations to change. One of his best customers was the wife of a top airline executive. In my memory, the airline was Trans World Airways, but it could have also been Pan Am or one of the large local carriers. The executive's wife was so taken with the quality of Raymond's work that she recommended him to her husband, who was looking for a company to take over reupholstering all the seats in the airline's fleet.

Raymond's income would have increased tenfold, but he turned down the offer because it would have meant hiring and supervising more than a dozen men. Needless to say, the rest of the family was crestfallen. In our minds, we already had a host of new things, from bicycles to cars to clothes. I pictured myself on a brand-new Schwinn bicycle, complete with headlight, horn, and plastic tassels. I'd use a playing card and clothespin, of course, to make it sound like a motorcycle.

But that bicycle dream would have to wait.

20
THE APPRENTICE

My father always spoke wistfully about W.B. Moses & Sons, the company where he got his start as an upholsterer, so I wasn't surprised to find a metal furniture plate in his treasure box. The plate is bent in several places along its length, and was probably pried off the frame of a sofa, chair, or chest that came his way for reupholstering.

If you lived in Washington, D.C., during the company's life (1861-1937), W.B. Moses & Sons would have been your first choice for fine furniture. A promotional brochure hawked the company as "the largest exclusively retail furniture, carpet, upholstery, drapery, bedding, and wall-paper house in America." Even the Senate Reception Room at the U.S. Capitol is fitted out with the company's custom-made benches of Flemish oak.

Raymond, still a young boy just out of third grade, his highest level of achievement, would set off each morning, lunch pail in hand, and make his way to the employee entrance of the company's building, which occupied the entire corner of 11th and F Streets, N.W. He would wend his way through the building, past the sewing section and into the upholstery shop, where he would report in with the master craftsman tasked with turning him into a real upholsterer.

He would learn about every available fabric and how each "behaved" in the creation of a finished piece. He would learn how to identify wood by its color and grain, and which stains and shellacs worked best with each. He would learn how to measure and estimate the materials needed for a job. And he would learn how to diagnose and correct underlying problems that hastened the need for reupholstering.

And he would learn perfection.

If he ever told me the name of the man charged with turning him into a fine craftsman, I have certainly forgotten it. But when he did speak of the man, which was not often, it was with a mixture of agony and admiration. The man held Raymond to the task, never settling for anything but perfection. There were hard lessons and times when Raymond would hold back tears as the man laid into him about any imperfection in technique or outcome.

But Raymond learned the trade, and learned it well. If it had not been for the Great Depression, I'm sure he would have had a long career at W.B. Moses & Sons. That was not to be, of course. As the economy tanked, so did the fortunes of W.B. Moses & Sons. Raymond was let go, and like many people back then, was "out on the streets," looking for work.

In Raymond's case, he was literally out on the streets. He and a friend would drive through the city each morning, looking for furniture put out on the street as part of an eviction. They would then take their "found furniture" and reupholster it from fabrics bought at deep discount from various supply houses, including the back door of W.B. Moses & Sons. They would then hawk the finished pieces door to door in the wealthy sections of the city.

It was hard work, and the profits were marginal, so Raymond jumped at the chance offered him one day to become a staff upholsterer at the Hotel Washington. And we know how well that turned out.

21
ALL THAT GLISTERS

My heart skips a beat as I pull the golden coin out of the treasure box. A bearded Spanish conquistador stares out at me from the face of the coin, which is stamped, "One Doubloon, Anno Dommini 1650." Could this possibly be real? And if it is, what is it worth?

I turn the coin over, and I have my answer. A pirate stares at me, a cutlass in one hand and a flintlock pistol in the other. I can just make out a pirate ship in the background, but then I see the sad truth that has been stamped on the coin: "Pirate Gold."

It is just play money, and you can get one today for about six dollars on Ebay. How this play money came to be seems to be a mystery. People are selling them, but none knows the back story of these brass coins. They could have been distributed by a cereal company (Captain Crunch?) or been sold in little faux leather bags at Ben Franklin's Five and Dime, perhaps as a set with a felt pirate hat and a plastic cutlass. I'm sure I would have coveted that.

Whatever the source, the coin certainly reveals Raymond's penchant for pranks. He must have known that his treasure box would be found one day, and that the coin would generate my exact response. I can see him chuckling as he places it in the box among the other coins.

Also, pirate gold fits perfectly with his handling of money, particularly the coins that fell his way from the cracks and crannies of his customer's furniture. It's not surprising to me that the handful of coins in the treasure box is all from foreign countries. He had other plans for U.S. currency.

Raymond worked on a lot of old furniture. Many of the pieces had been collecting coins and other odd bits since the nineteenth century. My father became a coin collector by default, and I was swept up in the hobby as well. I had several blue coin-collecting books for pennies, nickels, dimes, and quarters. The books had slots for coins from the 1890s to the 1950s. The idea was to fill every slot.

At the end of a workday, my father would bring in his collected loot, and the two of us would sort through the coins. We never found any rare coins, the ones that would transform our lives, but each find that filled a slot prompted a loud woot from me.

Raymond let me have any coin I wanted, except for his passion: silver dollars. Those would have been removed from the pile long before he came into the house. Despite our economic situation, he wouldn't part with them for any reason. They were his pirate treasure, and he treated them accordingly. I know this because I watched him bury a box of them one morning.

I was sitting in our kitchen, in the nook my father had built so he could enjoy a cup of coffee while keeping a sharp eye on his pigeon coop and the shop. My father, dressed as always in gray work pants and a blue flannel shirt, came out of his shop, carrying a wooden box and a shovel.

He set to digging, stopping every few seconds to make sure no one was watching. And then he carefully placed the box in the hole, filled it back in, and scattered leaves on top to camouflage the disturbed ground.

I've always wondered over the years whether the box was still there. I did a Google Earth search a few years ago to see if our house had changed in any way. The pigeon coop was gone, as was Raymond's shop and the lopsided metal garage he used to store old furniture.

I suppose I could try to be a returning pirate one night, and search the yard with a metal detector. Of course, I'd probably be shot by the current owner. And besides, I like the idea that some of Raymond's treasure is still out there.

The current owner might also be able to find my little blue books of coins. I didn't bury them, but I did hide them away in a secret place. When my father built the second floor to our house, he added a set of built-in drawers in the wall of each room. If you pulled the drawers out, you would have access to a space between the floor and the roof. I think that's where my blue books are now, along with a couple of science experiments I conducted by placing a wet piece of Wonder Bread into an empty peanut butter jar. Result: fuzzy.

22
HIGH SEAS DRIFTER

My father was a fisherman. I don't need to be reminded of that by anything in his treasure box, but an item comes to hand anyway. It is a token from the amusement park and arcade at Chesapeake Beach, our family's favorite summertime destination in the 1950s.

Chesapeake Beach had something for everyone. If you liked to play in the surf or walk, you could stroll into the bay and walk out almost a mile before the water rose above your knees. If you liked to eat, and could afford it, you could go to the Rod 'n Reel Restaurant and enjoy Crab Imperial. If you liked to swim, but didn't want to walk a mile, you could go to the beach's Olympic-sized pool. And if even that bored you, you could buy tokens and spend the day on their Ferris wheel, watch one-minute silent films in the arcade, or play bingo nonstop at the beach's bingo hall. And if none of that appealed to you, you could whine all day, along with my brother.

On any fine summer Saturday, you could see us climb into our maroon 1950 Plymouth and, after a seemingly endless drive and an excessive number of *are-we-there-yets* from my brother, pile out in the parking lot of Chesapeake Beach, where we would scatter. My mother would grab the picnic basket and trudge up a hill to the picnic tables, where she would spend the morning reading one or more romance novels before gravitating to the bingo hall, her enduring passion.

My sister, Nancy, was tasked with keeping a close eye on my younger brother, Kenny, which usually meant a trip to the pool or the arcade. If I had had my druthers, that's where I would have been as well. But my father had other ideas.

We had brought along our fishing gear, and the plan—Raymond's plan—was for us to go out on one of the charter boats and troll for Rock Fish or Blue Fish. All we had to do was select a charter boat, pay a fee, and climb on board.

The problem was all the charter boats were either already out on the bay or full-up for the next trip. Undaunted, Raymond selected the next best course of action: renting a motor boat. There, too, we ran into a slight problem. All the rental boats, the ones that came with powerful Mercury outboard motors, had already been rented. All that remained was an old rowboat with an engine no bigger than a toaster, an engine that made a little *putt-putt-putt* sound at full throttle.

Raymond laid down the cash, and we were off, though not at any great speed, the interval between one *putt* and another so comical that it provoked laughter among the men on the pier, who pointed at us as we made our way toward the bay and open waters. We were moving so slowly, I could watch a waiter move from the kitchen of the Rod 'n Reel to the restaurant floor, where he slowly placed heaping plates of food in front of a family of four.

I turned to my father, who was trying to coax more speed out of the engine. "Can we go to the Rod 'n Reel when we get back?"

Raymond quickly put an end to that dream. "No," he said. "We brought a picnic basket."

In my mind, I weighed the difference between butter-and-sugar sandwiches and Crab Imperial, and sighed.

"Why the heavy sigh?"

"Nothing."

I turned my back on Raymond and watched the prow of the little boat bounce in the light chop of waves as we slowly, slowly, slowly made our way to the magical place Raymond had selected for us to fish. When Raymond finally shut down the engine, dropped anchor, and began fumbling with his fishing rod, I turned around to see how far out we were. The Rod 'n Reel had disappeared from view and the shore was just a suggestion on the horizon.

Minutes later, we both had lines in the water, and I knew that it was only a matter of time before something went wrong. Every time I fished with my father, our lines would inevitably cross, creating a tangle that could only be undone with a knife. And with the tangle, came the harangue. It was my fault. I was a miserable no-account bastard. He should have known not to bring me.

This one-sided exchange would go on and on until Raymond had repaired his line and dropped it back in the water. As always, I refused to fish from that point onward, slamming my rod down on the bottom of the boat and turning away from him.

We sat in silence, Raymond waiting for his line to twitch as I stewed and watched the sun glint on the waves, which seemed to be getting higher and higher as the minutes ticked away. Finally, my father noticed the waves, and broke the silence.

"Looks like we have some weather coming in," he said, cranking at his reel to pull in his line. "Let's get back to shore."

Raymond set his rod aside, pulled in the anchor, and began pulling on the cord to start the little engine, which could not even manage a single *putt*. He tried and tried again, but it soon became apparent that we were dead in the water, a plaything for the waves and the current, which were growing rapidly and pushing us farther out into the bay. And then the rain began, near torrential, pushed sideways by the wind. Visibility dropped to near zero.

And then I saw it. A dark shape bearing down on us, large and looming, and getting closer by the second.

I shouted at my father, who was trying to get the oars locked into position. "Freighter!"

Raymond turned, and the whole world slowed down. He screamed something at me, but I couldn't hear. Then, in a final act of desperation, he turned to the engine and gave the cord one last violent tug. It started! Just like in the movies!

He beckoned me to take over the tiller to the engine, so he could grab the oars and row. How we managed to pass by each other in the little boat without falling into the six-foot waves was a minor miracle. But we managed it, and were soon at work, Raymond rowing frantically as I kept the boat at full throttle and pointed it away from the path of the freighter, which finally slid by us about fifty feet away and disappeared into the rain.

After an hour, the waves began to subside, which was apparently the signal for the little engine to offer its last *putt*, and die. We were still way out in the bay, and couldn't make out any landmarks that made sense to us. Another hour passed, and another. Raymond continued to row, but how he knew which direction to row remains a mystery to me.

Finally, at dusk, we could make out the lights of the Ferris wheel, which would serve as our lighthouse as we rowed slowly to shore, where we were greeted with tears and hugs by our family, an officer from the U.S. Coast Guard, the manager of the Rod 'n Reel, and a small crowd of beachgoers and fellow fishermen.

In a show of kindness and generosity, the restaurant manager offered us a free dinner, which we gladly accepted. It was the first time I had ever had Crab Imperial, and it seemed like the food of the gods.

23
OOH-LA-LA!

Raymond was not a traveler, but he delighted in every foreign coin that fell his way. If he were here now, he could probably match each coin with the piece of furniture that had offered it up. He would tell you the customer's name and what she looked like—particularly if she was pretty—and what importance the coin may have had for him.

Raymond's treasure box contains sixty-seven coins from twenty-two countries, covering the period 1870-1988 (*See* Appendix for full list). The oldest coin, and probably the most valuable of Raymond's coins, is a copper 10-centimo coin struck in 1870 by the Spanish Provisional Government during the Spanish revolution of 1868-70. The newest coin, a 1988 Canadian 10-cent piece, is significant only because Raymond would have been at least seventy-nine, and still working, when he dropped it in the box.

I'm not sure whether any one coin held my father's interest for long; the fact that they were foreign was enough for him to plunk them into his box. Still, there are at least two interesting coins in his collection.

25-Centavo Centenario de Martí (1953)

This Cuban coin marked the centennial of the birth of José Julián Martí Pérez, 1853-1953, a Cuban poet and essayist who was also an important revolutionary philosopher and political theorist. Known as the "Apostle of Cuban Independence," he became a symbol of Cuba's fight for freedom from Spain in the nineteenth century. This coin was struck during the reign of Batista, in the same year that Castro launched his own revolution.

1-Centavo Filipinas (1944)

When I first pick up this coin, I think it is American. One side is clearly marked "United States of America." In the center, there's a shield topped by an eagle. American, right? But then I flip it over to see it just as clearly marked, "Filipinas," with the image of a bare-chested leader and an active volcano in the background. Two and Two come together at last and the coin presents itself as a coin struck when the Philippines was a U.S. territory. Someone must have thought highly of the coin, or the country, because there's a hole drilled in it for use on a necklace.

And then there were the less notable coins, the ones that had darkened to black or been worn down by time, their countries of origin, years of issue, and denominations nothing more than ghostly ciphers. One coin, a small copper one, was as thin as a communion wafer, with edges as sharp as a razor.

Neatly folded under the pile of coins was a 5-franc note issued by the Banque de France in 1943. A young teenaged girl in short-shorts comes immediately to mind.

My job on Raymond's visits to customer's homes was to fetch and carry, and otherwise to remain silent and unobtrusive. But sometimes a customer would spot Wallpaper Lenny shifting his weight from one foot to the next, looking bored, and offer him something to eat or drink. As hungry as I was—always—I had been instructed by Raymond not to accept such favors. I think he thought it unprofessional.

At any rate, this particular customer was the wife of a French foreign-service officer. Raymond could barely contain his "appreciation" for her beauty, and especially for her disarming French accent. The look on his face suggested that he was witnessing some new wonder of nature.

She turned to me and smiled. "Oh, my poor boy, you look so lonely and forlorn."

"No, I'm okay."

She shook her head. "No, no, no, you must meet my daughter."

"Um," I said, giving it my best shot at an intelligent response as I looked at my father for help. But he was too busy ogling her to pay me any attention at all.

"Come with me," she said, grabbing me by the arm and leading me into the next room, which she referred to as their library.

"We have many books. Please have a look while I get Marie."

She turned and left the room, leaving me with a floor-to-ceiling, wall-to-wall shelf of books, most in French and most dealing with history and diplomacy. As I ran my finger along the leather spine of a treatise on economics, I could hear her in the other room, calling up the steps for her daughter, who answered back in an even thicker French accent.

Moments later, Marie came bouncing into the room and gave me an appraising look. Was I worthy of her attention? Apparently not. She nodded at me, and then turned and left the room.

Seconds later, she was escorted back into the room by her mother, who gave her a final little push back into my presence. "Now, Marie, talk to the boy. Practice your English."

The mother turned and left, leaving the two of us in silence. Marie was angry, and pouting, and I was having a hard time taking in how beautiful she was.

She picked up on that immediately, and gave me a sly smile. Yes, she would practice her English, but she would also practice her feminine wiles. I was a test case for her. How would I react when she winked? When she walked? When she tried erotic pose after erotic pose?

Apparently, my raging hormonal trance gave her every reason to believe that she had mastered femininity and allure. And I certainly wouldn't have argued with her. It was my first exposure to ooh-la-la and I was loving it.

24
BAUBLES, BANGLES, BRIGHT SHINY BEADS

If the contents of Raymond's treasure box are any indication, he may have been more blue jay than pigeon. He had a penchant for bright, shiny things, and value was apparently never his true north. I sorted the things he brought back to his nest into two piles, one for men's things and one for women's things.

The men's pile is dominated by a collection of tie clasps. I can see Raymond reaching into the box to retrieve any one of them to hold down the pre-knotted tie he wore with his estimating suit. Two are very plain, gold-tone affairs that got the job done without drawing attention to themselves. A third features a single tiny blue stone at its tip to add a touch of class. A fourth features a large, flamboyant, faux pearl for those times when Raymond would be estimating at the home of a wealthy customer. The last tie clasp is clearly not Raymond's, though. It features a bass-relief image of a Cessna-type airplane. Whoever wore it—perhaps the airline executive I mentioned earlier—wanted everyone to know he owned and flew his own personal plane. Raymond did not.

Next come the belt buckles, one engraved with an "R" for Raymond, and two others, one engraved with an "S" on a black enamel crest, and the other engraved with "LJW." Another black enamel crest engraved with the letter "W" appears to have popped off its buckle, which is nowhere in evidence.

There are some odd bits as well. A gold ID bracelet with no name, a keychain with an attached foreign coin dated 1864, a pendant of the McGregor coat of arms, the stirrup of a watch buckle, a star-and-crescent enamel pin, and something Raymond never had enough money to make use of: a money clip.

Dominating the women's pile is a gold-tone necklace, with a pendant locket big as a walnut and seemingly made of lead. Any woman who wore it would have suffered neck strain halfway through the party. She might have also taken advantage of the locket's true purpose, a freshening dab or two from the locket's interior reservoir of perfume glacé. The maker's mark inside—Avon—indicates the necklace was surely owned or hawked by the Avon Lady.

Next up is a heavily tarnished silver-chain ring topped with a curved ID plate engraved with the name "Bobbie." It barely fits on the tip of my pinky, so I think Bobbie must have been a petite young lady. I doubt that she would have been able to wear the next item, a silver bracelet with four evenly spaced faux pearls. It even fits my wrist, so I think the woman who owned it was more substantial than little Bobbie. But don't fret, Bobbie, there's another bracelet that seems to have been made just for you. It's a gold-rope bracelet with a broken clasp.

There's also a silver sweater clasp, the gold buckle of a woman's watch, a small gold chain, a long silver-tone chain, a long gold-tone chain, and a blue plastic teardrop pendant. Five clasp-style earrings complete Raymond's collection of women's jewelry: a simple gold hoop, a large silver-rope hoop with a clasp that suggests Art Nouveau, a delicate gold earring with four interconnected gold bangles shaped like flowers, and the three-bead remains of a pendant earring.

I don't know why Raymond chose these baubles for his treasure box. Perhaps he could match them with their female owners, and kept them as trophies to remember them by. Of course, you'd expect that sort of thing to be the work of a serial killer. But my father was nothing more than a serial upholsterer, a blue jay of a man who collected baubles, bangles, and bright shiny beads.

25
LOUISE'S ASHES

I reach for Raymond's treasure box, and I see him doing the same thing, except it's years ago, back in the 1960s. For safe keeping, he keeps the box on the top shelf of his bedroom closet, out of bounds for the likes of me. He has learned that from experience, because we both well remember the time I found his French postcards in his dresser drawer as I was searching for Christmas presents. That was quite a Christmas.

He catches me looking at him, and waggles a finger at me. "Don't you dare. Don't even think about it."

He turns back to the closet and pushes a small blue box aside to make room for his treasure box. I know it well. The little cardboard box contains the ashes of my Aunt Louise, my mother's one-year-older sister.

And then Aunt Louise is pulling up next to me in her old Hudson Hornet. Sleek and aerodynamic, the car looked like it was racing at full speed even when it was parked. And so did Aunt Louise. Where my mother, Dorothy, was shy and demure, and given to plain dress, her sister, Louise, was the polar opposite: outgoing, outspoken, flamboyant and flirtatious as all get-out. A *tease*, my father would say.

"Whatcha doin'?" she said, rolling down the window, a curl of smoke rising from the cigarette dangling from her ruby lips. It's 1959. She's a vibrant, sexy forty-two, and I'm a 16-year-old boy with raging hormones, a fact she knows full well and uses to tease me at every opportunity.

My friends immediately stopped tossing our football around, and came up beside me. From their expressions, I could tell that, like me, they were in dropped-jawed hormonal thrall of the beautiful strawberry blonde staring back at them.

What we were doing was playing a pickup game of street football, but I wasn't quite sure anymore. "Nothin'," I said. "Football, I guess."

She gave my friends a nod and a wink. "Hi, boys, how's it hangin'?"

My friends were now bug-eyed. A herd of elephants could have run by, and they wouldn't have noticed. There was only Aunt Louise and their thoughts of what she might say or do next. And the smell coming from the car, a heady blend of floral perfume and cigarette smoke, was intoxicating.

She gave a little laugh, and turned her attention back to me. "C'mere, I wanna show you somethin'."

I took a tentative step forward, as did my mesmerized friends.

"Not you, boys," she said, shooing them back with a delicate flick of her hand. They complied, moving back a few steps and huddling up to whisper about her.

I took another step closer to the car.

She blew out a puff of smoke. "Lenny, come closer. You'll never see my new shoes from way over there. I can't believe I found them in your shithole of a shopping center in Coral Hills."

I walked closer, into her cloud of cigarette smoke and perfume. When I got within her reach, she grabbed my shirt and pulled me up against the car door.

"Nice shoes, huh?"

I looked down, but it took me a while to notice the shoes. She had her dress hiked up over her silky thighs because of the summer heat, and her pink panties drew me in like a beacon.

"Ain't that sweet, Lenny?"

"Huh?"

"The shoes, darlin', the shoes."

I looked away from the center of the universe and looked down at her shoes. They were red patent leather with four-inch heels. My father had a name for them, too: fuck-me shoes.

I remember gasping for breath, unable to form words.

Nothing got by Aunt Louise. "Are you all right, honey?"

I nodded and somehow found a word. "Yes."

And then she caught me looking. "Oh, my," she said, pulling her dress down over her knees. She laughed with that deep smoker's laugh of hers, and then gave me a wink. "Don't you dare tell your momma about this."

I nodded absently.

She let go of my shirt, releasing me back into a changed world. "You should get your momma shoes like this."

"Uh-huh."

She looked past me at my friends, who continued to gawk at her. "You play nice now, boys."

And with that, she threw the car into gear with a crunch, and lurched away, a cloud of smoke and perfume trailing behind her.

That is the lasting image I have of her. I know very little else. I know she was born in 1916, but I don't know when or how she died. I do know that she married and had three children: Sonny, Skippy, and Herbert. I also know that Skippy (age 4) and Herbert (age 5) drowned in the Anacostia River, close to the Sousa Bridge, while playing on a sandbar, there brother Sonny (age 11) unable to save them. I have a clipping of a photograph from a 1940 edition of *The Washington Star*, showing my Uncle Earl, Louise's husband, consoling Sonny outside the ninth precinct station of the Washington Police. Aunt Louise was just 24 when this happened.

I also know where to find Louise's ashes. They're in *my* closet now, sitting next to an old fedora. Over the years, I've wondered about possibly spreading her ashes somewhere, but the somewhere escapes me.

26
COUSIN BUDDY AT THE BAT

As the opening credits roll, the camera, at ground level, follows a man walking quickly but deliberately down a city sidewalk. We see only his shoes—black Italian loafers, probably Lorenzo Banfi's—for six, seven, eight steps, then the camera slowly begins to pan upwards. We see the trousers of a black Armani suit. The camera rises, we see an aluminum briefcase, then the gloved hand that holds it. The camera rises farther, to the man's face. It is the contract killer, code name "Cousin," played by Christopher Walken. The camera follows him as he enters a doorway, takes an elevator to the fourth floor, jimmies the lock to an empty office, opens the briefcase, assembles a sniper rifle, specifically a .308 caliber Walther Commando P-126 with a Maxsight 3000 laser sight, moves to the window, raises the rifle, and fires one quick round between the eyes of a drug lord who has just emerged from a restaurant across the street . . .

This is the image that invariably comes to mind whenever I tell my friends about my cousin, the contract killer. The problem is, everyone's first thought is *professional* contract killer. That was not my Cousin Buddy.

Let's roll the camera again, starting at the feet and working our way up. We see steel-toed black work boots. Not that Cousin Buddy was much of a worker; he just liked what these boots could do in a bar fight. There is no Armani suit, either. Think soiled gray trousers held up by a pencil thin white belt that Cousin Buddy also used from time to time as a whip. If you're guessing now that he'd be wearing a dirty tee shirt with a pack of Lucky Strikes rolled up in one sleeve, you'd be half-right. Cousin Buddy smoked Camels.

You probably would have missed the tattoos, though—a coiled snake on the right biceps and a large anchor on the left forearm, both from his brief time in the navy—because the tattoos were not what drew attention to Buddy. What made people stare, sometimes at their peril, was the deep triangular indentation in Cousin Buddy's forehead. As Cousin Buddy usually put it, "Never anger a woman with a flatiron in her hand." Cousin Buddy had come at her in a drunken rage, and she had picked up and thrown the first heavy object that came to hand. The point of the iron had penetrated to a depth of about an inch, leaving a pit shaped like an equilateral triangle, or better yet, a perfect home for a tiny pyramid. Why it hadn't killed him outright is still a mystery to me. But it was certainly a subject of conversation, stares, and—inevitably—fights.

Cousin Buddy was someone you didn't want to mess with. At 6'2" and 270 pounds, he was no Christopher

Walken. If I were casting the role today, I would probably go with John Goodman.

"Stay away from your Cousin Buddy," Raymond often warned me. He didn't like anyone on my mother's side of the family, particularly "that beer-swilling, good-for-nothing scoundrel" Cousin Buddy. But for a 14-year-old, a warning is often an advertisement for adventure, so I spent more than a few afternoons at his house, particularly at times when Raymond was on a rampage for something I had done or hadn't done. I could always seek asylum at Cousin Buddy's house, and the house was only a couple of blocks away, easy to run to in any real or imagined emergency. Most times, I'd play catch with him and his friend, whose name escapes me, both of whom were big Washington Senators fans. Both had autographed baseball bats. I forget the names of the players who had signed them, but Cousin Buddy and his friend loved those bats.

Just saying the words "Cousin Buddy" was enough to make most grown men run for cover, but he had always been good to me, teaching me knife skills with his switchblade, including a game where you splayed the fingers of your hand on a table and the other player stabbed at the space between each finger as rapidly as he could. I wasn't much good at it, but he was. If blood was spilled, it was usually his.

One evening, as Buddy and his friend sat in a neighborhood bar, they were approached by a stranger who offered them $500 if they would kill his wife. My cousin would later admit in jail that he really thought this was a great opportunity for him and his friend to finally hit it big. He liked the sound, the cachet, of "professional contract killer." He had hoped that this first murder would just be the beginning of a new and profitable business.

But things went wrong.

Cousin Buddy and his friend accepted the man's offer, went home, grabbed their baseball bats, and went to the address the man had given them. When they busted down the front door, the wife was sitting at a card table, playing solitaire. Cousin Buddy never talked about what happened next, but the newspapers reported her bludgeoning death the next day. They also reported the capture of Cousin Buddy and his friend. The woman's screams and the smashing sounds had alerted the neighbors, who had immediately called the police. Cousin Buddy and his friend were picked up minutes later as they walked down the street, their prized but bloody bats still in their possession.

Buddy's friend hanged himself in his holding cell the next day. Cousin Buddy was convicted of murder and received a life sentence, as did the husband. Cousin Buddy was anything but a model prisoner. Any chance he may have had for parole ended when he knifed and killed a fellow inmate. He died in prison in 1998.

27
GOTTA LIGHT?

The next item out of the box is a small, black leather case with a gold clasp. It's slightly wider at one end than the other, and all its corners are rounded. It looks like a case for a musical instrument, but at just three inches long, it is definitely not that.

I open the clasp and lift the lid, and there it is: an elegant cigarette holder resting on a form-fitting blue velvet lining. Its mouthpiece is made of a black plastic-like material, perhaps Bakelite, and it's fitted to a white meerschaum receiver for the cigarette. Halfway up the receiver's length is a carved band of roses. It looks as pristine as the day it was made, but when I shine a flashlight down into it, I can clearly see a buildup of nicotine and tar. Someone used this, but kept it in its case most of the time.

The holder may have come to Raymond as a right of salvage, but I immediately think of three people who could have pulled off the panache required by a cigarette holder.

The first is my Aunt Louise, who would have had no trouble adding it to her repertoire of coquettish charms. I can see her sitting at a bar in her red heels and a matching dress. One hand is on her hip and the other holds the cigarette holder aloft, swinging it in a soft arc as if to beckon a champion to light her cigarette. The words are already forming on her lips. "Gotta light?"

The second candidate is my mother's other sister, Georgia, known by everyone as Aunt Georgie. Barrel-chested and gruff, with a personality to match, she would be sitting, not on a barstool, but in her royal blue wingback chair, looking every bit the empress of her living room. Picture Winston Churchill in a flowered dress.

The third candidate is one of our neighbors back then, Mr. Estes. Time has made me lose his first name, but I could never forget him. He and Raymond shared a somewhat contentious over-the-fence existence. Raymond didn't like the way Mr. Estes' son, Lenny, played his drums outside, scaring the pigeons. And Mr. Estes didn't like the way Raymond's pigeons left calling cards all over his lawn chairs and the roof of his house.

Other than that, the two families were the best of friends. And for a brief period when I was twelve, Mr. Estes' daughter Frances and I shared a spin-the-bottle crush on one another.

But back to Mr. Estes. A drinker and a heavy smoker, he was the polar opposite of Raymond. I see him even now sitting in his living room chair, engulfed in a cloud of smoke coming from the cigarette in his mouth and a just-finished cigarette in his ashtray, which is filled to overflowing with the butts of dead Pall Mall cigarettes.

But it's not the fact that he's smoking that draws my attention. It's how he's smoking. The cigarette is pinched in the grasp of the hook that serves as his right hand. I can definitely see him making use of the cigarette holder. He would take a puff, swing his hook to the side, and waggle his eyebrows at me. A sip of beer and a burp would soon follow.

28
A GRAVE EVENT

The next item out of the box comes in its own black leather case, stamped with the name of the manufacturer, "Mabie Todd & Co. Makers." Resting inside on a burgundy velvet liner is an elegant nineteenth century dip pen. Its tip and ferrule are 14-carat gold, and its finely tapering handle is mother of pearl. There is a thin "build-up" line of royal blue ink inside the scoop of the ferrule, indicating that the user regularly dipped into an ink well one inch deep.

How this dip pen came to be in Raymond's box is a mystery. It could have been an heirloom passed down in the family. Or it could have been an item scooped up from a customer's sofa, according to Raymond's Third Rule of Salvage.

If it is an heirloom, any suggestion that it would have been passed down in some loving, civil way, from one Boswell to the next flies in the face of all I know about Raymond's competitive, avaricious brothers and sisters. A memory comes back quick and hard.

My family and I are standing at Grandma Daisey's gravesite, watching her pearly white coffin being lowered into the ground. Raymond's brothers and sisters and their families are there, too. Words are said from a black book by a man dressed in black. Tears are shed.

But then, as the coffin hits home with the finality of the grave, Raymond's brothers and sisters disperse, quickly. They seem to be speed-walking to their cars, much to the dismay of Raymond, who is lingering at the grave to whisper his own words and toss in a handful of dirt—ashes to ashes, dust to dust.

We slowly walk back to our car and drive from the Virginia graveyard to our home in Maryland. As soon as we get in the door, the phone starts ringing. It's Raymond's brother Stanley. Raymond's eyes grow wide, and he slams the phone down in its cradle.

"Back in the car," he shouts. "They're stripping your Grandma Daisey's house."

It takes us an hour to get there, my father spitting nails the entire way. "Bastards! Bastards!"

Stanley meets us on the front steps with two words: "Too late."

The house has been stripped of furniture, rugs, and paintings. Even the attic has been emptied out. All they seem to have left behind is Christmas ornaments, which my sister, Nancy, scoops up and spirits away to our car. Odd bits, the things no one wanted, are scattered on the floor. It's possible that in the chaos, the little pen fell to the floor and went unnoticed, only to have my father discover it in the aftermath. I'd like to think that happened, that it was Daisey's pen. Raymond would have then at least had something to remember his mother by. But that's where memory fades to black. All I can remember is my father standing in Daisey's living room, crying.

29
LET US PRAY

The large round medal is silver-plated and tarnished, so it takes me a while to decipher the inscription above a bas-relief image of Jesus giving comfort to two poor people: Ut Unum Sint, "that they may be one." A depiction of the Vatican is on the flip side, so it doesn't take too much research to determine that the medal was struck to celebrate the Roman Catholic Jubilee of 1975. That holy year was apparently one of forgiveness of sins and also any punishments due to sin. Reconciliation, if you will.

To Raymond, the medal would have been no more than a curiosity. Our family, at best, could be described as fallen-way Methodists, with the exception of my sister, Nancy, who converted to Catholicism and practiced her religion devoutly until her dying day.

Not so Raymond. The idea of sitting in a church pew surrounded by strangers singing hymns he could only mumble was not his idea of fun. And it would have definitely felt claustrophobic to him. No, he would much rather spend his Sundays with his pigeons.

My mother was more religious, but only to a point. I'd call her a near-Methodist, a believer in god, but not much of a churchgoer. She did help out around the church, though, and for many years was tasked with setting up for the communion service. She would sometimes take me along with her on a Saturday night to help lay out the wafers and grape juice for the next day's service. And we always had a supply of the wafers at home, which made a pretty good snack when topped with peanut butter.

She tried her best to interest each of her children in the church. "It's only a couple blocks away. You should go."

There were at least two problems with that. First, we didn't want to go. And second, we never really had "Sunday best" clothes. Going to church was always an exercise in humiliation.

Still, she persisted. And, in the end, money did the trick. I remember her putting a few coins in my hand for the collection plate and nudging me out the door. I would dutifully go to the church, but only to be recognized by someone who could report back to my mother that I had, in fact, attended church.

Once the services began, however, and everyone's attention was on the minister, I would sneak out of the church and make my way to the White Rabbit, a diner just two blocks away. There, I would deposit my tithe on the counter, thank god for a donut and a cup of coffee, and worship Elvis on the jukebox. Eventually, I would spot just-released churchgoers heading for the diner and its fried-chicken Sunday special. That would be my signal to make a quick exit. If I timed it just right, my mother—and more importantly, Mrs. Kite—would see me heading up the street along with other neighbors heading home from church.

30
FOR YOUR AMUSEMENT

The little brass token, about the size of a nickel, depicts a horse's head and the words, "Ray's Track." My first thought is the token is a promotional piece from one of the local race tracks: Laurel, Rosecroft, maybe even Charles Town. But then the memory comes galloping into view.

The token is not from a racetrack, but *for* a racetrack. On those rare occasions when Raymond hit it big at the track using his sure-fire, can't miss, change-your-mind-at-the-betting-window method, he would treat the family to a day at an amusement park, usually Marshall Hall or Glen Echo, both of which are gone now, lost to history and video games.

Raymond would give me and my brother and sister a handful of change that we could spend any way we wanted. He would release us into the park while he and my mother proceeded directly to the penny arcade. My mother would focus on machines that offered short silent movies featuring Little Nell and Simon Legree.

Raymond would go straight to the cash-to-token window and exchange cash for a handful of Ray's Track tokens, the only tokens that would work on this electro-mechanical horse-racing machine invented by the Bally Company in 1936. Pick your horse based on the pre-race odds and watch as nine tin horses race down the track. Your winnings: more Ray's Track tokens.

While Raymond stood there, screaming encouragement and disgust at the tin horses, I would be working my way through hot dogs, cotton candy, candied apples, candy corn, and almost anything edible I could stuff in my face. Once sated, I would then use my remaining money on the many rides: Merry-go-Round, Ferris wheel, Tilt-a-Whirl, and finally, The Whip.

The Whip, as you might imagine, involved sitting in a rotating car shaped like a clamshell. The ride would take you in a circle, and the car would whip around suddenly at a designated point in the ride. The combination of spinning at great speed while being whipped around was something my little brain just couldn't handle, as the crowd waiting their turn to ride soon found out. The expression *lose your lunch* comes to mind.

I would spend the rest of the day sitting under a tree that I'm sure was less green than me. Hours would pass, but finally, after Raymond had all but exhausted his supply of Ray's Track tokens, saving one as a souvenir, the family would reunite at a designated time and place.

On the ride home, my brother would boast about his skill in knocking down tenpins with a baseball, my sister would lick quietly at the candied apple she had saved just for the trip home, and I would sit there with my eyes closed, hoping to die.

Meanwhile, in the front seat, my father would rail at the dastardly inner workings of the Ray's Track machine, that the "whole thing was rigged." My mother would nod quietly, lost in her own thoughts the rope-wrapped Little Nell and the oncoming locomotive. *Damned Simon Legree!*

31
A TOKEN OF MY APPRECIATION

There are twenty-seven tokens, badges, and medallions in Ray's treasure box. (*See* Appendix for full list.) We've already discussed several of them, but five more stand out.

The first that comes to hand looks like a military service ribbon at first glance. An ornate bronze badge hangs from a military-style ribbon featuring vertical olive bands left and right, with a royal blue band down the middle, separated from the olive bands by very thin stripes of blue, yellow, and red.

As much as it looks like an award for gallantry or service, it is just a ceremonial badge from the 36th National Convention of the American Legion (1954). Raymond never served in the military, even though he was just thirty when World War II began. The nervous breakdown he'd experienced following the elevator death of his friend and coworker was enough to disqualify him, much to the relief of my mother.

But for Raymond, the disqualification was humiliating. He felt that he had been unmanned and had to suffer through the whispered comments of neighbors and the suspicious, judgmental eyes of his customers. Anger and frustration boiled within him and erupted out of him without warning and without limits. When I came along in 1943, dealing with the expense of a new baby, as well as its needs and demands, just added to the fire.

Living stateside during the war was a struggle for every family, and the little red token in his treasure box is clear evidence of tough times. It's an OPA (Office of Price Administration) Coin valued at one red point.

Raymond would have received it in 1944 or 1945 as change when he used ration stamps to buy a variety of rationed goods, including meats, canned goods, sugar, coffee, gasoline, and more. The tokens could then be used in future transactions for rationed goods.

In those years there were thirty different red tokens and twenty-four blue ones. All were made of pressed vulcanized fiber and were just half an inch in diameter. Hold a single piece of popcorn in your hand and you'll get a good idea of their weight. In the grocery store, you would have used blue-point tokens for processed foods and red-point tokens for meats and fats.

Many retailers used tokens as change back then. They didn't want you to take ten cents in change and spend it somewhere else. So the next token I pull from Raymond's treasure box is not surprising.

It's a brass token about the size of a nickel. On one side, it says, "West Wyoming Hotel," and on the other, "Ten Cents in Trade." You could use this coin during your stay for meals, newspapers, and many sundry items. Not surprising at all, but what is surprising is the curve thrown by the name of the hotel. When I first picked it up, I immediately thought of a hotel in the wilds of Wyoming. Further research, however, revealed that the token came from a now-defunct hotel in West Wyoming, Pennsylvania.

I'm certain my father never stayed at the hotel, but maybe the person who did was taken there by the man behind the Licensed Chauffeur Medallion I pull from the box. The octagonal silver-toned badge identifies license holder number 15859 for the year 1922 in wild, wonderful West Virginia.

As a current resident of West Virginia, I find it hard to imagine a big market for chauffeurs, but the medallion says otherwise. I know Raymond would have loved to be driven around in a limousine. Coincidentally, 1922 was the year that the Armbruster Stageway Company of Fort Smith, Arkansas, built the first stretch limousine. Having Raymond in the back seat of one would have been a stretch, of course, particularly at age thirteen.

Raymond was not that lucky, but he *was* superstitious enough to carry the most unusual token in his treasure box: a "Magic Mystx" good-luck coin purported to protect the bearer from evil spirits. My father never walked under a ladder or stepped on a sidewalk crack. When our cat gave birth, the black one was quickly given away. And Friday the Thirteenth was always a day to stay indoors and avoid tempting fate by anything that might happen in the outside world. He was a man who believed in fairies, ghosts, angels, and leprechauns.

And as I lay the unusual coin aside, a new memory suddenly comes to mind, sparked by the word *unusual*.

32
A MOST UNUSUAL THANKSGIVING

Raymond tried his best. He really did, but the food being served to him by my new wife, Ruth, was not to his liking. No, he actually hated it.

Raymond was a man of simple tastes and simple food. If food was seasoned with anything other than butter and salt, it rarely found favor with him. And this was true even more so when it came to Thanksgiving.

To Raymond, Thanksgiving was an overcooked turkey, oyster dressing, canned cranberry jelly, mashed potatoes, and string beans. Period. Ruth, on the other hand, had something more exotic in mind. She wanted to impress my parents with her cooking prowess, so the first thing she had to do was roast the turkey to perfection, which meant that for Raymond it was, in his words, *unusually* moist.

She had prepared candied sweet potatoes, which were *unusually* sweet and not mashed potatoes at all. She had prepared her mother's recipe for cranberry sauce, a piquant blend of cranberries and oranges, which were *very unusual* to Raymond. With a nod to Baltimore's Polish community, she had prepared a wonderful version of sauerkraut involving currants, which Raymond sensed were definitely not out of a can or a jar, as they should be, and therefore *unusual*.

Raymond's eyes lit up when he saw something familiar in a bowl—green beans—but then noticed brown slivers of something mixed in.

He pointed at the bowl. "What are those?"

Ruth set her fork down. "Oh, those are green beans with toasted slivered almonds."

Raymond turned to my mother. "Look at that, Dickie. So *unusual*."

My mother nodded back. "I've seen those before, but only in a magazine."

To top off the meal, Ruth had prepared a stuffing like no other, adding chocolate chips to the mix. Clearly a bold choice that Raymond found to be *unusual,* even though he loved chocolate.

And so the meal progressed, one unusual dish after another.

"How do you like the stuffing?" I said to them.

My mother, who was more skilled in polite conversation, said, "Oh my, it's wonderful."

"What about you, Dad?"

Raymond kept chewing for a few seconds, which was not unusual for a man of seventy-one who had just two teeth left. "It's so . . . *unusual*."

Ruth defended her bold choice. "I thought the chocolate chips would make it more like a Mexican mole."

Raymond blinked, hard. "A what?"

Ruth started to explain, but was saved by my mother. "Well, I think it's quite delightful. Well done, Ruth."

Ruth nodded, set down her fork, and stood up. "Is everyone ready for dessert?"

I could see the anxious looks on my parents' faces. What sort of *unusual* concoction would Ruth be serving next?

Her words put them at ease. "I hear you like pumpkin pie and mincemeat pie. We have both."

My father beamed. At last he would be able to eat something familiar. "With canned whipped cream?"

"Um, no," said Ruth. "I made the whipped cream myself."

My father slumped back in his chair. "How *unusual*."

Still, Raymond was able to slide the whipped cream off his pie with a fork, and enjoy his plain pumpkin pie.

Then, after a cup or two of *unusual* coffee, he and my mother were out the door, rumbling away in his old Ford Econoline van.

I turned to Ruth. "What did you think?"

She started to giggle. "I thought it was *unusual*."

I can only imagine the conversation between Raymond and my mother on their ride home. I'm pretty sure he would have replaced the word *unusual* with something that honestly described his feelings about the food. Then he would have probably said something like, "I'm still hungry. Let's stop at the Dixie Pig."

Ah, Dixie Pig, home of *usual* barbecue.

33
FA-LA-LA-LA-LA

The tattered, almost tinsel-like tin foil Raymond used to line his treasure box is a reminder that Thanksgiving invariably leads to Christmas, that time of year when every emotion possible comes roaring out of Santa's sack. A host of memories spring to mind . . .

I am eight again, tugging on shoes too small and holey mittens warmed overnight on the living room radiator. I have already donned two pairs of pants and my only three shirts to brace myself against the cold. My mother appears beside me, young and pretty as always, insisting that I wear my Christmas scarf, a scratchy abomination as long as an anaconda, knitted loosely and tightly by my Aunt Louise, using a geometry known only to her. Despite my protests, she wraps Scarf Louisienne around my neck several times and nudges me toward the front door.

Outside, the world is white and still, the only sound the whisper of the falling snow. I lift my head to the snowy heavens, stick out my tongue, and accept winter's cold communion.

Come, we have much to see.

Oh, Christmas Tree!

Every family has its own unique traditions when it comes to Christmas trees, and it was no different when I was growing up. Mrs. Kite, who lived directly across the street from us, always had a blue spruce just tall enough for her knitted white angel to forever bend at the waist, its head and back scraping the ceiling. There were no ornaments on her tree, also a tradition, and only blue lights. The Armisters, our better-off friends, preferred artificial, flocked-white trees, with white ornaments, and white lights, for their pale homage to Christmas. That's just how they rolled.

And then there was our tree.

Shaggy, gangly, too tall, too wide, of suspect species, our tree stood, leaned, or floated in the corner of our living room, held in place by defective tree stands and poorly engineered guywires to create a state of tenuous stability. And yes, I said floated. That was the year our tree stand died, and Raymond came up with the brilliant plan of suspending the tree from the ceiling, which had the novel effect of making the tree rotate, first to the right, until the rope knotted tight, and then back to the left, gathering speed as it turned, a victim of whatever air currents were handy.

I remember our cat Sylvester watching the rotating tree intently, one paw raised, ready to bat at the swirling ornaments, then running for cover when the tree reversed direction and headed back his way.

Ah, the ornaments.

If you could make them, we had them: paper chains, strung popcorn, cutout cardboard figures of gingerbread men or angels or steam locomotives—anything our scissors imagined. Real candy canes and cookies baked with string loops were also a must, and provided our first meal on Christmas morning.

Did you have glass ornaments? Yes, a few, and none the same, and most collected from yard sales by Raymond, who had a deft eye for disturbingly grim ornaments, particularly glass Santas that looked more like gargoyles than jolly old elves, or large globe ornaments of a color reminiscent of the La Brea Tar Pits.

What about lights? Oh, we had them, at least for those brief hours when all the bulbs functioned properly. Nothing as fancy as the Armister's lights, those bubbling candle lights that forever bubble in my memory as Mrs. Armister, thin as a pin, puts another paper roll in their player piano, which did its best to play a few carols as we sipped hot chocolate from tiny china cups. No, we just had standard lights of all colors. Raymond would start at the bottom of the tree and make a spiral of lights as he worked his way to the top. If he had planned correctly, the last light would glow at the top of the tree. Some years, it was the middle of the tree, though. And one year, he had a clump of lights left when he reached the top, so he just hung the clump at the top. Raymond believed in kismet when it came to Christmas tree lights—wherever they ended up, they ended up, and far be it from him or anyone else to change that. It was just part of the ineffable magic of Christmas.

Did you put tinsel on the tree? We called them icicles, and they were made of thin strips of tin foil, and it was the job of me, my brother, and my sister to put them on the tree. My sister preferred to separate the icicles into separate strands, then consider each strand's proper place on the tree, then place the strands just so, so that the draped icicle was of equal lengths on both sides. My brother and I opted for rapid deployment of the icicles, tossing them by the handful at the tree, from various angles and distances, in more of an "icicles happen" approach. Any that fell to the floor during this process would be scooped up, along with dust and cat hair, and be tossed at the tree again, until the tree was loaded. Then one of us would climb the open stairs behind the tree and top it off with our one-winged angel, Gladys. And then the tree would be officially complete.

Some years the tree was perfect and magical. Other years the tree look cluttered or sparse, or seemed to be the victim of gale winds, ornaments akimbo, blown to one side. And in still other years, the tree resembled an old man weighted down by layer after layer of colorful rags. But they were our trees, and we loved them all.

When did you put up your tree? Always on Christmas Eve, which is when we'd either buy a tree, at a greatly reduced price, or cut down a tree in the woods at the bottom of our street, although that sometimes meant tying several small scraggily trees together to create a bushier tree.

And how long did you leave your tree up? The tree went up on Christmas Eve and came down on New Year's Eve, according to my mother's wishes and Raymond's deep superstitions. He thought it was bad luck to have two Christmas trees in the same year. Besides, with trees so beautiful, so magnificent, so magical, who could bear such intense orgasmic joy for more than a week?

A Christmas Totem

I can still see the thin layer of snow and hear it crunch under the soles of my Roy Rogers galoshes as Raymond and I crouch-walked through the woods in search of a Christmas tree. It was Christmas Eve and, unlike previous eves, when we invariably picked up our tree for next to nothing, or nothing at all, at a nearby Boy Scouts lot, this Christmas Eve had not gone well. The lot had been picked clean of all but a few handfuls of pine needles, and the boy scouts were tearing down their camp and dousing the fire that had warmed them the last few weeks.

Not to be deterred, Raymond had come up with a Plan B, prefaced with a string of obscenities aimed at no one in particular. Finally, he had shouted, "We'll cut down our own damn tree," his voice rising, the force of "damn tree" causing the scouts to back off and scatter. In my memory, I clearly recall one of them shouting for a "Mr. Beasly," no doubt the scoutmaster, but Mr. Beasly was nowhere in evidence, so the boy had stood there, flapping his arms and shouting, "Oh, shit, oh shit!"

And with that we returned home to collect a saw and flashlights before trudging down the hill to the woods that marked the end of civilization.

We trudged. And we trudged, the cold insinuating itself into my galoshes, through the barrier of newspaper I had wrapped around my feet for warmth, into my ankles, spreading up to my knees, at which point, in frustration, I laid my first F-bomb on my dad, urging him to quit the search.

Raymond just stared at me blankly, as if the F-bomb could not possibly have come from my lips, then grunted, picked out three scrub pines at random, not a one with a trunk thicker than a big toe, and sawed them down.

"We'll make do," he said.

I started to protest, but the cold had crept up my thighs and was threatening to reach higher, so I just nodded, grabbed hold of one of the little trees, and started dragging it toward home, not even looking back to make sure my dad was still with me.

Once there, I dropped the little tree outside and raced into the house, which had the welcome warmth of a blast furnace. As I recuperated in the kitchen with cocoa and over-baked sugar cookies, I could hear my father dragging the trees inside to the protests of my older sister—"that's not a tree!"—and the bawling of my younger brother, who was given to tears several times a day back then, often without reason.

"Well, it's not a tree now, but it will be," Raymond said.

And it was, in a way, although not in any way that would suggest "Christmas Tree." Tied together with twine, the "tree" was more like a piney bush, as wide as it was tall, with limbs shooting this way and that, but not in any way that would suggest the work of nature. Not even Charlie Brown could have imagined such an abomination.

My mother laughed at the tree every time she looked at it, but then, she was that kind of woman, laughter being her antidote in times of stress and hardship, which always. I and my brother and sister had a different response, which could euphemistically be called "grumbling," mostly under our breath, for fear our father would hear us.

Trimming the tree made matters worse. Loaded down with tinsel, it looked like some shaggy, tinseled yak. That's when my brother began to cry again, inconsolably, drawing the attention of my mother, who came into the room, took one look at the newly decorated tree, and actually went beyond a laugh, even beyond a guffaw, to some unnamed form of laughter that could only be the stuff of legend.

And that's when things went terribly wrong. Raymond—let me be kind—lost it, rushing into the room, grabbing the fully decorated tree, and throwing it out the front door and down the steps, where it would remain until Easter as a cautionary totem for our neighbors in general and our postman in particular, his pace quickening as he walked up to the mailbox, deposited the mail, and fled.

In his defense, Raymond claimed that his actions were not only unavoidable, but justifiable, because we didn't have the Christmas spirit, although those were not his exact words. And perhaps we didn't.

And yet, whenever I think of a heavily tinseled yak, I invariably think of Christmas.

A Christmas Mashup

The table was set, like it is now, but this was years and years ago. My mother was rushing back and forth from the kitchen to the dining room with platters and bowls of food. Not in abundance, mind, because if we were in the middle class at all, we were there just recently, and barely.

The fact was Raymond had just delivered a sofa and two chairs back to a customer, who had paid in cash, making Christmas dinner not only possible, but a feast by our standards, which meant a meat other than price-reduced hotdogs would be involved. Our typical meal of beans on Wonder Bread, or sometimes Wonder Bread on top of beans, would be replaced by a fine ham, fresh green beans, apple sauce, mashed potatoes, and fresh-baked biscuits. There was even a rumor of pumpkin pie.

Let me be clear from the start. Meals in our home were always a matter of competition. The faster you got to the table and the faster you ate, the more likely you would be to get the calories you needed to make it till the next morning. Some people we knew actually dined, taking a leisurely approach to meals. We fed. Quickly, ravenously, covetously. My mother, rightly, thought we'd all make fine zoo animals.

My brother and I were the chief competitors, and had perfected the fine art of grab, snatch, and gobble, which invariably left my older sister sitting in front of a plate with a single slice of bread on it, and nothing more.

Needless to say, the prospect of such a glorious meal was weighing heavily on me and my brother as we sat in the living room, waiting to be called to the table. If you had seen us then, you would have sworn that we were deep in thought, dealing with a problem in astrophysics, but we were actually formulating our plan of attack. Should the ham slices be grabbed with our hands or speared with a fork? Should we use one hand or two to grab the biscuits? Would dumping the entire bowl of green beans on our plate be appropriate? Did we care?

Countermeasures were also in play. When I'm called to the table, should I throw a body block at my brother, or perhaps throw his chair away from the table, leaving him to compete for the spoils standing up? Should I create a diversion, say, throwing his Lincoln Logs across the living room?

All this, and more, was on our minds as we sat on the couch, poised for our assault, our finely honed feeding reflexes at the ready. There was one concern, though. There was a rule, a rule we dared not disobey, and that was never to attack the food before Raymond had loaded his plate. I think he enjoyed the game as much as we did, or so we thought, because he would sometimes load his plate slowly, holding the final spoonful over his plate for several seconds, looking back and forth at us, before depositing the food on his plate and saying, "There," which was our signal to commence our feeding frenzy.

Call it fate, call it providence, call it whatever you like, all our battle plans went out the window when our cat, Sylvester, chose the moment we were called to dinner to launch his own attack, on our Christmas tree, racing up the trunk and grabbing my mother's handmade silk angel with his teeth, toppling the tree on his way down.

My father, mother, and sister ran for the living room to give chase. My brother and I, on the other hand, had worked ourselves into such a fine state of dinner readiness that we launched ourselves at the table, grabbing food left and right, stuffing it into our faces. By the time the rest of the family appeared, there was not much to see but culinary devastation.

Incensed, Raymond picked up the half-empty bowl of mashed potatoes and threw it up against the far wall of the dining room, shattering it into a million pieces and leaving a distinctive splat of mashed potatoes behind. Guilty as charged, my brother and I were summarily sent to the upstairs bedroom we shared, where we were imprisoned until morning. Our thought process back then was not so much that we were being punished, but that we were being punished before dessert. I think my brother even said, "Wait, you mean without pie?"

As wrong as we had been, my mother refused to forgive my father for throwing the mashed potatoes against the wall, destroying her one piece of good china. He, in turn, refused to clean it up, so the splat remained as a symbol of greed and pride and obstinacy for us all. And so it stayed, year after year, growing crustier with age, like each of us.

When we sold the house fifty years later, after my mother's death, the mashed potatoes were still there, a yellowed crusty splat on the dining room wall. The buyer thought the splat looked like the kind of lichens you'd see on a rotting tree stump.

Back then, though, when we were young boys, my brother thought the splat looked like a flattened reindeer. My sister, the peacemaker, who sought to mollify us all, was adamant that it looked like nothing other than a large wonderful snowflake. Raymond, when asked, would just look away or rattle his newspaper in front of his face. My mother would just say, "Don't get me started."

To me, it looked like the kind of splat I'd see when my snowball missed Percy Williams and hit the brick wall he was hiding behind. But now, when I think about it, I see that little splat of mashed potatoes as a symbol for each of us, all of us, a mashup of what it sometimes means to be a family just trying to make it through to the next day, moving forward from one Christmas to the next, ever struggling, ever dreaming, never more than a splat away from who knows what.

Now, could someone please pass the mashed potatoes?

On Daisey's Pond

The first thing I notice about my sister's Christmas tree is the display under it, which was passed down to her by my Grandma Daisey. It's a mirror, surrounded by spun cotton to create the look of a frozen pond, on which several antique lead figures skate: a young boy in red mittens, his little sister (or so we always imagined) trying to keep up, and a man and woman skating close together arm in arm, young lovers all bright and smiling and having the time of their lives, along with their dog, who stands along the edge of the pond, afraid of the ice but eager to join them, and barking his head off for all eternity.

I pick up the young boy, and I am back in my grandmother's living room, years and years ago, sitting next to her Christmas tree, looking at this very display and surveying the room, which is filled with aunts and uncles and cousins galore. And, of course, there is Grandma Daisey, positioned in a chair in the center of the room, so people could kiss her when they arrive and kiss her when they departed.

In my memory, Grandma Daisey sits there still, anchored to her chair, all but oblivious to the swirl of her children and grandchildren and who all else knows has come willingly or been dragged to the annual Christmas event at "granny's house." She is a small woman, with silver hair done up in tight, tiny curls thanks to a home permanent kit applied just this morning by her daughter

Bessie, the middle child of her thirteen children, who has also done her up in a flowered dress more appropriate for spring, and topped that off with a red Christmas sweater featuring holly berries and reindeer. Her dress is not long enough to cover her stockings, which end in thick rolls just below her knees, revealing skin that is parchment white.

Bessie has placed her in a chair at the center of the room, as always, and as Daisey sits there staring blankly into space with her head and arms resting on freshly pinned antimacassars, she looks more like a display than a woman who has endured seventeen pregnancies and a life in the rough and tumble of near poverty with an alcoholic husband who took the strap to her when he had a mind to, despite the efforts of her sons, my father included, to stop him.

She does not speak, but she is listening, intently, as her daughter Ruth, the oldest and her caretaker, opines nonstop on how her government department has gone to hell since she retired.

"Nincompoops," she says, jerking her clenched fists up in front of her chest in a way that suggests she could snap their necks and think nothing of it.

Daisey blinks her ice-blue eyes, but more out of boredom than alarm. Ruth is being Ruth, and Daisey just wants her to stop for once and not natter on and on like she was Queen of the May, which she thinks she is, no doubt about that.

I glance around the room. Uncle Ira and Aunt Mae are sitting on the couch next to me, along with their daughter, Dorothy, who is trapped within herself, unable or unwilling to speak. Beyond them is the long dining room table, chock-a-block with food and surrounded by my many aunts and uncles, including my Uncle Fred, the redheaded uncle, the "milkman's kid," who is red-faced and pounding the table to make his point in an argument with Raymond that arises every Christmas, only the topic changing.

At this point, I usually retreated to Grandma Daisey's bedroom at the back of the house, where many other cousins could be found, all in the throes of boredom, biding their time until their parents had had their fill of food and conversation, and made their excuses to leave, most wanting to "make it home before dark," which would invariably lead to a rapid exit of all but a few aunts and uncles and their tribes.

Daisey's small four-poster bed wasn't big enough for more than a few kids, so most of us sat on the floor, some sitting quietly, others bragging loudly about the treasures they had received from Santa. I always sat in front of the small bookshelf next to her bed, which contained the complete works of Charles Dickens, bound in leather with gilt-edged pages that smelled of death. I would pull out a volume and start reading.

"It was the best of times, it was the worst of times, it was the age of wisdom, it was the age of foolishness, it was the epoch of belief, it was the epoch of incredulity, it was the season of Light, it was the season of Darkness."

I would read more of it to you, but at about this time, my mother would always appear, my coat in her hands, sending a clear message that we were leaving, Raymond eager to get home before dark. We would make our way back to the living room, lean into the cloud of lavender that surrounded Grandma Daisey, and dutifully peck her on the cheek.

"Do you remember it?" my sister says, startling me.

I smile up at her and put the little skater down on his frozen mirrored pond.

"Oh, yes, especially Uncle Fred."

She rolls her eyes at me. She remembers, too.

The Junkman's Christmas

Raymond collected junk. A lot of junk. If you were thinking of having a yard sale or a garage sale, the first rule of success was to let my father know the date and time, because he would be there, and all those things you thought were worthless, including that ceramic thing with one leg that sort of looked like a giraffe, would be scooped up by my father for display in our home, which the neighbors referred to as "the yard sale that moved indoors." Out of earshot, of course.

One of his greatest finds, to his mind, was a Santa figure about a foot tall. Under its felt and plastic skin rested an evil mechanism that in full battery was designed to proclaim "Ho-Ho-Ho, Merry Christmas!" as it raised its arms to indicate a successful field goal.

He had picked it up at a yard sale hosted by the Armisters, our wealthy, or at least better-off, neighbors, who were all about battery-operated devices, but who exercised one of the privileges of wealth, discarding perfectly good items out of boredom, which they referred to as "ennui."

Of course, this particular Santa was not in perfectly good condition. No, it was more like a severely emotionally disturbed Santa. Instead of saying, "Ho-Ho-Ho, Merry Christmas!" it said, in the best of my ability to interpret, "Ho-Ho-Hotcha" followed by a screeching sound so disturbing it made small children and pets scatter for cover. The sound, accompanied by Santa's fixed, insanely gleeful expression and slowly rising arms, made you feel like some demon from hell was coming for you.

Once Raymond realized its effect on people, he used it year after year to unmercifully startle and scare people who came by the house at Christmas, particularly my friends. By the third Christmas, most of my friends refused to come into the house without assurances that the Santa was nowhere about.

"Is it?" they would say. Just two words, and I knew exactly what they meant.

"Yes, but my father's taking a nap, so it's safe."

Then they would come in, and there the Santa would be, sitting on the mantle of our fake fireplace. My friends would shudder upon seeing it, and then we'd race to the relative safety of my bedroom, where we would play until it was time for them to go home. Even then, they made me escort them out of the house for fear that the evil beast would jump out at them before they made it to the front door.

Raymond had weaponized Christmas.

And so it continued, year after year, until that one Christmas when not even fresh batteries could coax it to life. The neighborhood rejoiced at the news, but my father, who was given to dark moods, just sat all day in his chair in front of the television, fiddling with the on-off switch, replacing or jiggling the batteries, checking the wire leads and solder points, and all but performing emergency surgery on his now mute Santa. It could still raise its arms, but without its terrorizing shriek, it was really just a pathetic assemblage of felt and plastic.

The next morning, Santa was nowhere to be found. My father had retreated to his workshop to upholster a client's sofa, and my mother refused to talk about it.

"Let's just say it's gone, okay?"

"But—"

"And whatever you do, never ask your father about it."

And then she had turned back to her work at the sewing machine, which whirred and rumbled all day in my memory as she helped my father by sewing up cushions and sofa skirts and whatever else needed sewing.

The Santa was never seen again. One rumor was that my father had given it to his best friend, Romeo Labona, who had a knack for fixing electrical devices, but once the next Christmas passed without the reappearance of the Santa, we all knew that it would never return to terrorize the neighborhood. America was safe once more.

Even so, even now, I make it a point to steer clear of the Christmas decoration aisles at our local drug store, for fear that I'll come upon a nicely boxed Santa with a "try me" button you push to hear it say, "Ho-Ho-Ho, Merry Christmas!"

I advise you to do the same.

A Christmas Bicycle

Our bicycles began to pick up speed as we raced down the hill, Tony on the left of me, Luigi on the right, all of us cranking hard at the pedals, each determined to reach the bottom first. I glanced quickly at Tony, who was looking back at me, bug-eyed. . .

My eyes had gone bug-eyed earlier in the day, when I had trudged slowly down the stairs from my bedroom, not expecting much in the way of Christmas presents. It had been a bad year for Raymond's one-man upholstery business, one of many, so the last thing I was expecting was what I had actually asked for: a bicycle!

It wasn't new, but it was in pretty good shape for a ten-year-old Raleigh English Racer. The 3-speed gears worked, the brakes seemed okay, and the leather seat was like new. There were scratches, of course, but the maroon paint still gleamed, as did the stainless steel air pump on the diagonal frame bar. It even had a little leather satchel attached to the back of the seat, which I soon found held a few rusted wrenches and a Pep Boys inner tube repair kit that had apparently never been used.

The only thing that looked odd about the bike was the fenders, which were made of an off-white fiberglass rather than metal. I guess the idea was to lighten the bike, making it marginally faster, which I hoped would help me win a race or two with my friends.

There were no other presents for me, other than a few pieces of candy in my stocking, so I quickly got dressed, threw a couple of grape sodas and quickly prepared peanut butter sandwiches into the satchel, and headed out to give my new bike an all-day try. That's when I discovered that Tony and Luigi had each received brand new bikes for Christmas, both of them remarking how sad my bike looked compared to theirs, which had heavily chromed fenders, headlights, horns, and plastic tassels streaming from the hand grips.

Of course, what they didn't have was multiple speeds like my bike. Theirs were traditional American one-speed bikes, with rear-only brakes activated by slamming back on the pedals—useful for leaving skid marks, but not as refined as the front and rear caliper brakes of my English racer. I didn't think they'd stand a chance against me, so the game was on! First one to the bottom of the "R" Street hill, the steepest hill around, would reap a shiny quarter from the other two, enough to pay for the new Burt Lancaster movie that had just opened, with a bag of popcorn to boot.

If I had thought about it, I would have unloaded the satchel, which because of the sodas, had drooped down to rest heavily on the fender, causing it to scrape lightly against the rear tire from time to time. But there just wasn't time. The race was on!

We positioned our bikes in the road, using the rear bumper of Raymond's old Plymouth as the starting line. The finish line was already a given—the horizontal bump in the road at the bottom of the hill, which marked the path of the underlying culvert that allowed our little creek to flow by. On a snowy day, the bump would have signified that you had made it down the hill alive on your sled. Despite our wishes, there had been no snow the night before, so the hill lay before us, steep and dry.

After some discussion about how to start the race fairly, Luigi just started a countdown from three to one, and we were off, Luigi taking the early lead as I fumbled to switch gears from first to second. By the fifth or sixth revolution of my bike's wheels, I had made it into third gear and began to steadily close the gap, my speed building quickly, houses and trees beginning to blur, my cheeks beginning to flutter the way the cheeks of test pilots fluttered in a centrifuge.

We were all going fast—too fast. If we had had any sense at all, we would have stopped pedaling and just coasted down the hill, but fifty cents was fifty cents, so we kept pedaling, the bottom of the hill quickly approaching as we raced side by side, the lead going back and forth.

That's when I had glanced at Tony and seen the bug-eyed look he was giving me.

"Fire!" he shouted at me, pointing behind me. "You're on fire!"

I turned my head to take a look, and sure enough, the back of my bicycle was ablaze, flames and smoke billowing from the satchel and the fiberglass fender.

I slammed on the brakes. Unfortunately, I applied more pressure to the front brake than the rear brake, so the bike flipped into the air, tumbling forward, me and the bike parting company during the second revolution, the bike crashing in flames to the ground as I bounced once and splashed into the creek, the water dousing the fire I hadn't known about, on my winter coat, which continued to smoke for some minutes as I slowly stood and checked for broken bones.

Tony helped me out of the creek and up the bank to the road, where we found Luigi already enjoying the rights of salvage, sipping at the one grape soda that had survived the wreck. Flames continued to lick at the satchel and the fender, which had melted onto the road.

"That was something," he said.

If it had been a different era, we would have stood there shaking our heads, going through every possible inflection of "dude." But it was the 1950s, so we just stood there shaking our heads.

"She-it," said Tony, looking down at the twisted wreckage. The handlebars were twisted around, the frame was bent, and neither wheel would ever make a circle again.

"It's not so bad," I said, swatting out the remaining flames with my cap and lifting the bike up, tugging at the handle bars to get them going in the right direction.

"You'll need new wheels," said Luigi.

"And a new frame," said Tony.

I nodded, recognizing what I was pushing back up the hill: a dead bicycle.

Years later, after my mother's death, I was sorting through the contents of the house. I found the bicycle where I had left it that Christmas morning—in the basement, propped up against a wall, a little piece of Christmas ribbon still attached to its handlebars.

I remembered the look on my mother's face that morning as I had dropped the twisted bicycle at her feet, and she had pulled me close, still smelling of Christmas cookies, trying her best to console me. There was sadness, and compassion, and the knowing look of a woman who knew, as I did, that there would be no replacement, no repairs. And that my father would no doubt have a few choice words for his no-account bastard of a son. Christmas would have to wait another year, and there would never be another bicycle under the tree.

I looked down at the bike and gave the front brake lever one last squeeze, a smile growing on my face. I thought then as I think now: we are all memories.

34
ONE FINAL MEMORY

The last treasures in Raymond's box are three ancient and yellowed stick-and-apply stickers promoting Disney characters. The first shows the impish cat Figaro trying to coax an obviously female fish named Cleo out of her fishbowl. "Wanna come out and play," he says.

The next sticker shows Mary Poppins lifting off the ground as the wind catches under her umbrella. "What energy crisis?" she says cheerfully. And the final sticker shows hound dogs Napoleon and Lafayette with a bone. Lafayette says, "Napoleon, how do you pull a bone-a-part?"

None of these stickers brings back a single memory of Raymond, but they do bring back memories of my recently departed sister, Nancy, a woman who loved stickers, glitter, and balloons until her dying day. When I came along in 1943, Nancy had already been Raymond's little princess for five years. Pampered and doted upon, it was only natural for her to welcome me into the family with loving grace.

Well, no, that's not actually how it went down. My mother actually caught her in my room one morning, trying to break my baby legs by pulling them out of the crib and twisting them this way and that. Fortunately, she eventually warmed to the idea of Baby Lenny, and became in many ways my best friend and champion.

If I have any storytelling skills at all, I'm sure I learned them on rainy days, playing paper dolls on her bedroom floor. All the windows in the house were closed against the rain, so there was no way for me to make noxious fumes with my hand-me-down chemistry set. Bored out of my skull, I would go to Nancy's room, where she would already be well into an elaborate plot with her paper dolls. She was always the hero, usually a princess from some exotic land, albeit a flat, two-dimensional one who looked like a bobbysoxer in a cute sweater and a crinoline-puffed skirt.

Whatever the story or convoluted plot, I was always the same character, "Bob the Boozer." My job was to somehow insinuate myself into the story and move it in unexpected directions. Sometimes I was heroic, knocking out some horrible cad out to despoil the princess. Other times, I was the villain, stealing her jewels and cash and making off with them on a moonless night. And sometimes I would just be lurking, inserting remarks now and then as Nancy charged ahead with her story.

We continued this form of play even into our adult years, without the paper dolls, of course. Anyone who has shared a table with us at a wedding would tell you that we were a formidable comedy team, with the wit and oddball banter of comedians like Bob and Ray.

But back to the stickers. Every year at my birthday and every major holiday, I would receive a letter from my sister that was easy to spot. The outer envelope would be covered with stickers and little hand-drawn characters perfect for the occasion. Pumpkins for Halloween, turkeys for Thanksgiving, candy canes for Christmas, and a variety of birthday cakes and candles for my birthday. I'm sure many of the letters made the day of our postman.

Inside, there would always be a card with loving thoughts, stickers, and hand-drawn hearts, usually with an equally bestickered letter and a photograph of her growing family of children and grandchildren. The last letter came at Christmas in 2018, even though she was then in the hospital, dying. She passed on New Year's Day 2019.

I could say more about Nancy, including how slow an eater she was growing up. I swear she could torture a single pea with a knife and fork for over an hour. But I think any fuller story of Nancy should fall to her children and grandchildren, the absolute loves of her life.

For now, I will put the stickers back into Raymond's treasure box. Time to close the box, slip back on the blue ribbon Nancy surely used to mark its importance, and tuck it away in my closet, as Raymond would have done, next to the little blue box containing Aunt Louise's ashes. Perhaps it will be discovered one day by another treasure seeker, and reveal a completely different picture of Raymond, and me.

When I started this treasure hunt, my goal was to unbox Raymond, but I realize now that the hunting has unboxed me as well.

There. We are both free now.

AFTERWORDS

My wife tells me that the best way to work a jigsaw puzzle is to start with the corner and edge pieces, and then work toward the center. I'm not sure I've accomplished even that in my attempt to assemble the jigsaw puzzle that was my father, Raymond. For one thing, I have only shown the pieces that sparked some memory of him and his life. Other pieces I have kept to myself, pieces so jagged and off-putting that you would slam the book shut and toss it aside in disgust or fury. Other pieces are just missing, fallen under the table of life.

I'm sure that my mother, brother, and sister would have added many more pieces, and perhaps challenged me on some of the pieces I laid down. In the end, you have a puzzle partially assembled by a 78-year-old man who genuinely hated his father when he was growing up. It's hard to forgive my father for his emotional abuse of me and my brother, but the realization now, all these years later that he suffered from posttraumatic stress disorder forces me to do just that. I can only wonder how our lives would have changed if someone had set the family down, told us what was going on inside Raymond's head, and given us a treatment plan to follow.

In the end, I had to deal with an unnamed demon that possessed my father. Raymond was by turns kind, generous, and funny, but there was always a darker Raymond just around the corner, the PTSD Raymond, ready at any moment to pounce on me and my brother with an energy and ferocity that could be more than frightening.

But he was my father, and I know now that he tried his best, even though he often failed.

Today I choose not to focus on the darker pieces of the jigsaw puzzle that is Raymond. Let them fall off the table or be carried away by crows. Let me be the blue jay and focus on the shinier things, on Raymond as a child, running barefoot through the streets of Washington, D.C., chasing horse-drawn wagons and new-fangled streetcars. Let him burst from his boyhood home on a bright summer morning and race to the waterfront for his bracing swim in the crystal clear Potomac with his little friend Darla.

Swim on, daddy. Swim on.

Raymond Edgar Boswell (1909-1992)
Dorothy Harris Boswell (1916-1996)
Kenneth Steven Boswell (1946-2000)
Nancy Boswell Harmon (1938-2019)
Leonard Everett Boswell (1943-)

APPENDIX
TREASURE BOX CONTENTS

Women's Jewelry and Accessories
Avon perfume glacé locket and necklace
Silver clasp coiled hoop earring
Faux pearl clasp earring
Three-stone cut glass earring
Chain ring with engraved "Bobbie"
Bangle clasp earring
Necklace chain (silver)
Necklace chain (gold)
Gold coiled bracelet
Gold-tone necklace chain
Watch buckle (gold)
Watch belt clasp (silver)
Blue plastic pendant
Gold hoop earring
Earring piece
Gold-tone medallion
Silver bracelet with four pearls
Back of earring
Silver sweater clip

Men's Jewelry and Accessories
Men's Belt Buckle Ring (gold)
Men's bolo tie clasp
Gold money clip
Gold tie clasp with pearl
Lapel pin with McGregor coat of arms
Gold-tone tie clasp
Belt buckle with engraved "R"
Belt buckle with "S"
Belt buckle with "LJW"
Clasp pin of 1941 British Farthing
Gold-tone tie clasp with blue stone
Part of black enamel pin with "W"
Tie clasp with relief of Cessna Airplane
Gold tie clasp
Gold ID bracelet (blank)
Key chain with coin (unintelligible)
Part of watch clasp
Star and crescent pin

Currency
Brazil
10-Centavos coin (1967)

Britain
3-Pence Coin (1960)

British Caribbean Territories, Eastern Group
25-cent coin (1965)

Canada
1-Cent Coin (1931)
1-Cent Coin (1952)
1-Cent Coin (1958)
Two 1-Cent Coins (1968)
1-Cent Coin (1969)
1-Cent Coin (1963)
1-Cent Coin (1964)
1-Cent Coin (1965)
Two 1-Cent Coins (1966)
1-Cent Coin (1975)
Two 1-Cent Coins (1972)
1-Cent Coin (1973)
5-Cent Coin (1971)
5-Cent Coin (1975)
5-Cent Coin (1972)
10-Cent Coin (1973)
10-Cent C0in (1988)
10-Cent Coin (1978)

Cuba (Republica de Cuba)
25-cts Coin—Centenario de Marti (1953)

France
5-Franc Note (paper, 1943)
1-Franc Coin (1943) (Travail Familie Patrie)

5-Franc Coin (1949)
10-Franc Coin (1957)
10-Franc Coin (1958)

Germany (West)
10-Pfennig Coin (1949)
5-Pfennig Coin (1949)
5-Pfennig Coin (1966)
2-Pfennig Coin (1967)

Greece
2-Apaxmai Coin (1971)
2-Apaxmai Coin (1973)

Lebanon
2½-Piastries Coin (19?8)

Luxemburg
25-C-Mes Coin (1947)
25-C-Mes (1963)

Japanese
10-Yen Note (paper)
50-Yen Coin (1970?)

Korea
1-? Coin (no date)

Mexico (Estados Unidos Mexicanos)

20-Centavos Coin (1982)
10-Centavos Coin (1942)

Netherlands
25-Cent Coin (1964)
1-Cent Coin (1956)

Nicaragua
No denomination, No date

Peru
10-Centavos Coin (no date)

Philippines (United States of America)
1-Centavo Coin (1944)

Portugal
10-Centavos (1963)

South Africa
6-D Coin (1941)

Spain
Diez-Centimos (1870)

Turkey
5-Kurus Coin (1959)

United States

1-Cent Coin (1917?) very damaged

Unknown Country
50-? Coin (?)
Two 2-? Coins (?)
Black, unidentifiable Coin
Damaged Coin
Worn, unidentifiable Coin

Vietnam Cong-Hoa
10-Dong coin (1964)
1-Dong coin (1964)
Five 1-Dong coins (1960)

Tokens and Medallions
LOOK magazine savings medallion
Washington Redskins 1973 schedule medallion sponsored by Johnny Walker Red Scotch whisky
Union Pacific railroad "lucky piece" made from a sample of aluminum used in the new Union Pacific train built by Pullman Car and Manufacturing Corporation using Alcoa Aluminum
The National Turf Digest Medallion
Bicentennial Medallion of the United States (1776-1976)
Licensed Chauffer medallion, West Virginia, 1922
Sales Award medallion, Curtis Publishing Company and *The Saturday Evening Post*

Vatican Jubilee 1975 Medal UT UNUM SINT Pope Paul VI Commemorative Catholic Church

Good Luck Souvenir, Gun and Stage Coach Museum, Shakopee, Minnesota

"Ray's Track" token

Reader's Digest 52-cent savings token

Sales Tax token, State of Washington

Ten-Cent Token, West Wyoming Hotel

Bicentennial Medal, Birth of George Washington, 1732-1932

Car Fare Only token for Garden State Parkway

King Bourbon Medallion

One Doubloon Pirate Gold play money

Amusement Token, Chesapeake Beach

Presidential Coin, Rutherford B. Hayes

Two Amusement Tokens

"One Transportation Unit" token, GSA Region 3

Uncle Billy's amusement token

"Old Age Assistance" token, Oklahoma

OPA One Red Point

"Good for Free Game" token

Metrobus student token, 1973

Swastika good luck medallion

Miscellaneous

Bradbury Heights award with ribbon

Crossed Swords badge

Mabie Todd & Company Gold Ink Pen, No. 2

Meerschaum cigarette holder

Convention badge, American Legion 36th Annual Convention 1954

Waltham 17 Jewel Pocket Watch (without hands or back)

Disney cartoon stickers (3)

Tin/Aluminum foil box liners

Payment receipt ($60.00 to Suburban Trust Company)

OTHER BOOKS BY LEN BOSWELL

Fantasies:
The Cave of the Six Arrows

Simon Grave Mysteries:
A Grave Misunderstanding
Simon Grave and the Curious Incident of the Cat in the Daytime
Simon Grave and the Drone of the Basque Orvilles
Simon Grave and the Sons of Irony

Other Mysteries:
Flicker: A Paranormal Mystery
Skeleton: A Bare Bones Mystery

Memoirs:
Santa Takes a Tumble
Unboxing Raymond

Nonfiction:
The Leadership Secrets of Squirrels
Stick Figures: The Life and Art of Len Boswell

ABOUT THE AUTHOR

Len Boswell is the author of eleven additional books, including the award-winning *Simon Grave Mysteries*. He lives in the mountains of West Virginia with his wife, Ruth, and their two dogs, Shadow and Cinder.

Note From the Author

Word-of-mouth is crucial for any author to succeed. If you enjoyed *Unboxing Raymond*, please leave a review online—anywhere you are able. Even if it's just a sentence or two. It would make all the difference and would be very much appreciated.

Thanks!
Len Boswell